This book is to be re
the last date s

THE FLIGHT OF THE
EAST PRUSSIAN HORSES

BOOKS BY THE SAME AUTHOR

British Native Ponies
The Foals of Epona (with A. A. Dent)
History of Horse Breeding
Horses of the World (3rd edition)
Huntsmen of a Golden Age
Know Your Pony
The Seventh Continent
Silver Spring
Successful Showjumping (2nd edition)

Translations

The Asiatic Wild Horse
Cavaletti
The Horse Today—and Tomorrow?
The Long Way Home
The Noble Horse

THE FLIGHT OF THE
EAST PRUSSIAN HORSES

Daphne Machin Goodall

DAVID & CHARLES : *NEWTON ABBOT*

Translated from the third edition of Die Pferde mit der Elchschaufel *by Daphne Machin Goodall published in 1966 by Paul Parey, Verlagsbuchhandlung, Berlin and Hamburg. This English translation published in 1973 by David & Charles (Holdings) Limited with the permission of Paul Parey, Verlagsbuchhandlung*

0 7153 6061 2

Set in 11/13 Baskerville
and printed in Great Britain
by W J Holman Limited Dawlish
for David & Charles (Holdings) Limited
South Devon House Newton Abbot Devon

SAGITTA
(who fell near Danzig 27.3.45)

The fields have been harvested
And the air is like crystal,
Woods—gold, green and red—
Let their autumn leaves fall.
The neigh of a young horse
Sounds like a fanfare call,
The earth, too, smells today
Like potato-mould!

Beneath an oak tree
A tired rider rests and yields,
His greeting thoughts flow free
Back to his native fields,
Greeting a noble mare,
The count of comradeship
Who, quiet in foreign soil,
Sleeps—that was long ago!

The rider lies full-length,
His heart is tired and sad,
He hums the song of songs—
East Prussia's melody.
And as a child from crying
His eyes close heavy too,
Of green and golden fences
Dreams of hunting long ago.

A distant whispering sound
Swells to a thunder roar,
And loud a horn is blown,
The verge of the wood before.
The cry of the hounds comes near
Like a cry of joy,
And the earth can scarcely bear
The thunder of horses' hooves!

With noble courage seen seldom
Sagitta leaps over,
The mane of the mare shines golden,
Brings joy to the sleeping rider.
The red of his coat catches
The bright sunshine
And the stubble field is dewy
With pearls, like champagne wine.

Now the ditch is wider
He soon is far behind,
And now there seems to be
A grey stone wall.
The wall grows high, and higher
Behind a watery ditch,
The field comes near, and nearer,
And the first leaps well over.

Sagitta soared towards heaven
Right to the Golden Gate,
Close behind the rest of the gathering
Of man, and horse, and hounds.
Hallali! sounded quietly
And now the horn blew faintly,
The dreaming rider softly
Sang East Prussia's melody.

The man awakes from slumber
Under the old oak tree,
After this rider's dream
He is from worry free.
He knows: they ride above
The same as on the earth,
And that God has love
For rider and for horse!

BOTHO VON BERG

Translated from the German by Daphne Machin Goodall

Contents

List of Illustrations

11

IN TEXT

All photographs are by the author

CHAPTER ONE

In Search of the Trakehner

There is no enmity, jealousy,
Politics or war—amongst horses.
With pride they carry pleasure,
With patience they bear poverty,
They serve the rich, and the needy
Without discrimination.
They live in every land,
Amongst all people,
As servants and companions
Given by God to man.

D.M.G.

'WHAT THE position of breeding now is, and what the future has in store, no one outside the country can say.' What significance these words of R. S. Summerhays held, and they were to prove a challenge, for some time later the opportunity presented itself to me to go and discover, in the post-war years, what had become of the Trakehner—the famous breed of East Prussian warm-blood horses—to which he was referring. I suppose his words drummed around in my mind for several months, until I was visiting friends in Western Germany, and one day, someone remarked: 'Well, why don't you write about the East Prussian horses?'

13

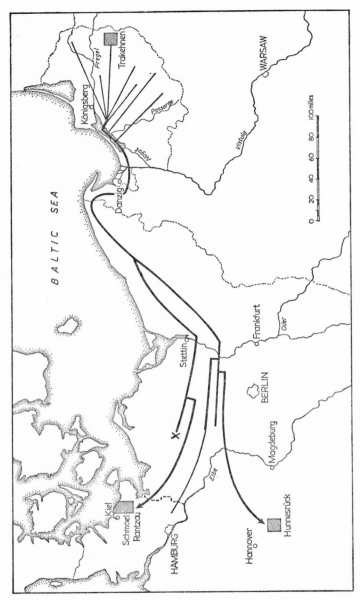

The trek of the East Prussian horses

Why then are East Prussian horses so especially interesting? Because they are the only breed of horses to leave their native land, and whose survivors have made one of the greatest and longest treks in history, enduring incredible hardship and suffering on a long, long flight in winter.

Many years ago, I stayed on an estate to the east of the Oder. It was a lovely countryside, with forests and lakes and rolling corn fields. And there I rode a little East Prussian mare, who was everything one could hope for in a riding horse. East Prussia was a very beautiful country, until it was torn apart by the ravages of war, the shelling and the bombing and all the other cruelties which accompany conflict. Its fields and its forests, its lakes and its seashores were conceived on a greater scale than one would find this side of the Oder. Estates ran to thousands and thousands of acres. The chief stud at Trakehnen of the East Prussian horse, and from which they derived their name—Trakehner—consisted of about 14,000 acres.

With the extent of their lands, so with their hospitality, which was proverbial. In England one is invited to tea, and one stays to supper: east of the Oder one was invited to dinner, and one stayed the weekend. I, personally, went out there for six months but received so many invitations I stayed another nine! East of the Nogat even an invitation for the weekend ran on into a month or more.

The scale of horse-breeding was run on the same lines, a man farming 500 acres, would have not one but probably five or more breeding mares, all with first-class pedigrees. A landlord with a large estate might well have a hundred or more horses running around the place, and perhaps he could travel by rail all day and never leave his own land. In Trakehnen itself, there were five herds, each containing around eighty to ninety horses.

15

But by far the greater number of breeding mares belonged to the smaller farmers, usually only one or two on each farm. They did all the usual work in the fields, often with their foals running beside them. Although some of the estates were large, the greater part of East Prussia was farmed, and the horses bred, by these small farmers. At least 80 per cent of the breeding lay in the hands of small breeders. The widespread idea that the breed was in the hands of big estate owners is not true. In 1919 a total of 56,777 mares were covered, then the number dropped in 1929 to 13,738, rising again in 1937 to 32,874. Of these mares about 20,000 were registered in the East Prussian Stud Book for Trakehner horses.

One can scarcely accept the vastness of a countryside with a completely cultivated agriculture, a flourishing culture, an ancient history, and so great a passion for horses. Of course, there are the enormous ranches of South America, and the vast plains of Siberia; but these are not farmed and they are not agricultural units in the sense that we understand it.

But the old way of life of East Prussia ended with World War II. Its people and their beloved horses were scattered westwards far from their native countryside. For this reason, the subsequent discovery of the East Prussian horse—the Trakehner—in Western Germany, involved quite a lot of travelling and research, as well as the pleasure of meeting and making many new friends; and the added thrill of piecing together shreds of information, which when I first received them, were as odd as the pieces of a jigsaw puzzle. It was only with the eyes of my friends east of the Oder, that I could even begin to visualise what pattern the puzzle was to take and what a beautiful, tragic picture would be shown, when the pattern was complete.

Page 17 (above) Mouse or dun-grey Tarpan yearling colt. Large herds were once to be found in the forests of Europe and the South Russian steppes; *(below)* the Marienburg, one of the largest fortresses in Europe, built by the German Order of Knights in about the thirteenth century

Page 18 The entrance to the Marienburg, still intact with knight and horse above the portcullis

I suppose in all the history of the world, there has never been such a tragedy as the attempted evacuation of the women, children and old people from East Prussia in 1945. Everything from man's inventions to nature was against them. Everything from Nazi Gauleiter's decrees to bombs, low-flying aircraft, ice, and at the most critical point, thaw, hindered, delayed and destroyed them. But amid the disaster and heartbreak of this great trek, there stood one positive thing: the courage of the horses.

I have tried to weave again the tapestry of East Prussia. Like a golden thread these horses wove their way into the Province and into the hearts of the many peoples of Europe who lived there—the little wild 'Schweiken', the armoured war-horse, the sweat-drenched gelding working in the fields, and the magnificent brood mare, a refugee also, who became the champion of all the brood mares of Western Germany. Truly they have shown us a monument of courage.

CHAPTER TWO

The Historical Background

BEFORE THE last war in most country towns of East Prussia, Silesia, Pomerania, or Brandenburg, one might see small, unremarkable brown or mouse-grey horses, even maybe, with a black dorsal stripe, standing tiredly harnessed in pairs to their carts, or perhaps tied to the back, chewing a little hay, whilst those carts were being unloaded. They had probably a long journey behind them, having come from a distance, pulling heavy loads of produce from a smallholding or a farm to the market. These farms lay at the back of beyond, and the way lay over cart-tracks and cobbled streets, and the horses quite likely had little food in their bellies.

In spite of this, however, they did not look overworked or starved. One of the remarkable things about them was that they were always in good condition in spite of the small amount of keep which their owners could afford to give them. They were never work-shy and scarcely ever ill, and because they were such economical feeders, they were really in every way the most reliable helpers of the farmers in those districts.

Similar horses to these were the old native horses of East Prussia, which, in all probability, were descended directly from the wild Tarpan. There is not much doubt that the

20

Tarpan were the ancestors of the East Prussian horse, who owes its hardness and stamina to these wild forebears, for the Tarpan lived in the forests and steppes, on very little food and in the roughest weather and climatic conditions.

The writer Friedrich Mager says that the Tarpan died out completely in Russia about a hundred years ago, but at one time this horse covered the whole of East and Middle Europe, decreasing his area until he occupied a south-easterly region in the steppes of South Russia, where he was to be found in ever decreasing numbers up to the middle of the nineteenth century.

The Tarpan had a fairly straight shoulder, but was finely made, he was usually mouse-brown or dun in colour, with a black dorsal stripe running down his back. Another writer Carl Stadie remarks that the little native Panje—pony of Poland, Lithuania, and Masuria—has inherited the mark of the Tarpan, the dorsal stripe, and this may be taken as a more than probable sign that they too are descended from the wild horse.

There is a very interesting story about the capabilities of the wild horse, for we are apt to think that they were never tamed, and only roamed around in herds in the forests or steppes, until their numbers were decimated either by natural causes or because the natives of these lands killed them off. This was not so at all. We know that there were three distinct types of wild horse: the diluvial horse, which was the ancestor of the European cold-blood or cart-horse type; the Tarpan of East Europe and West Asia; and the Przewalsky horse from the districts in and around Mongolia. In his book, *Über Pferde* (About Horses), Dr Bruno Dechamps describes an experience which the monk Wulfstan had when he visited the Pruzzens in East Prussia in the ninth century:

21

On the day that a funeral pyre had been erected for a deceased Pruzzen, who had joined his friends in the horseman's paradise, the funeral guests divided those of his belongings which remained over after drinking and playing, and laid them severally on the ground on the way from the man's house. Naturally the thing of greatest value was at the greatest distance from the house and of the smallest value quite near the house. Then the owner of the fastest horse in the country rode several miles distant and started a race for the legacies. So the fastest attained the biggest legacy and so on, until all the deceased's belongings had been reached, according to rank and power, since the fastest horse belonged to the highest in the land.

Up to the fifteenth century, bison and wild horses roamed over Europe and East Prussia, but they decreased rapidly and the wild horse was rarely seen after about 1600–1700. The last European Tarpan herds are to be found in reserves in Poland, and today in the forest of Popiellen (plate, page 17).

In the vast forests of East Prussia, there were various species of deer, wild boar, fox, badger, lynx, wildcat and to some extent wolves which came down from the forests in Russia; and of course, the very shy elk, which was usually to be found on its own, unless it was a cow with calf or at certain seasons. The writer Maurice Karkies saw a number of elk together under most unusual circumstances, which owing to their shyness can have been rarely observed before. One huge old elk stood on a tiny hillock, a herd of elk had congregated and were circling round and round to a regular beating of hooves, but presently they got wind of Karkies and vanished silently into the mists.

This unusual occurrence was later confirmed by an old

22

East Prussian fisherman, who, as a boy, had once witnessed a similar proceeding on the Frische Nehrung. Since the early history of the Province, the elk has always had a special place and therefore it is not surprising that the elk-antlers were used as the brand for the horses.

The geography of East Prussia lent itself to lawlessness and disorder and it was a constant thorn in the flesh to its more civilised neighbours in the West. When the knight Hermann Balk returned from the Crusades in 1231, he was asked by Prince Konrad of Masovia to take Knights of the Teutonic Order and to restore peace and to Christianise the native Pruzzens. These people were heathen, rode madly, as indeed did all the nomadic tribes, and they could put 30,000 mounted men in the field.

Heinrich Balk and his knights were successful in bringing law and order into the Province, and he and his successors founded a number of forts—burgs—including the architecturally beautiful Marienburg (now alas, a ruin), Insterburg, Georgenburg, and many others. The knights brought with them their heavy war-horses, which were partly descended from the Friesian and Ardennes heavy horses from Northern and Central Germany, and perhaps from Spain. Certainly these horses were of no especial type. Compared to the East Prussian descendants of the wild horse, they were considerably heavier and bigger, and to some degree, resembled the heavy working cob with which we are familiar from pictures of the knights of old, rather than a warm-blood horse. But although they had to be capable of carrying the weight of a man in armour, they also had to move fairly swiftly and have the stamina to travel long distances. So that these horses, through contact with the East where the Crusades had taken them, may also have possessed some Oriental blood.

23

In the early ages East Prussia was also one of the few Central European countries to have a very close connection with the British Isles. The earliest written record about horses in the Province is given by the already mentioned Wulfstan, the enterprising Anglo-Saxon who travelled there in the ninth century—and it may have been very much easier for him then, than it is for a present day traveller! In the fourteenth century the kings of England were politically and commercially interested in the country, so although we have no proof of it, visitors must have been coming and going in the intervening period, and told the Court all about it.

In 1391 Henry of Derby—later Henry IV—took between 300 and 1,000 men, and joined up with the Teutonic Order of Knights who were still occupied, as they had been one hundred years earlier, in stabilising the country. His ships put in at Königsberg—men, horses, armour, and every comfort including beer and wine. Also fine linen, furniture, and household goods were landed. To go to war in those days, with a knightly order, was looked upon as a kind of sport and it was attended with a certain amount of light-hearted festivity, much as the monarchs of a later day feasted before a hunt. One can imagine the colourful activity going on in the port of Königsberg as the young prince's horses disembarked, good substantial weight-carriers but probably short in the leg and not much above 15.2hh. From that day on there was a close connection between the two countries.

Henry stayed in the country several weeks and having laid seige to and conquered a town, he then returned home. On the journey back, we are told, he took with him several Latvian women and boys, two of whom he later sold for one mark. The price of a good horse in those days was four marks. Henry returned to East Prussia the following year but it seems that he had a difference of opinion, and so only stayed three days before going on to Venice, which had become the centre of the Teutonic Order, when the Holy Land was lost to them in 1291.

There grew up quite a British community in Elbing where a very good beer was brewed, and a rather large village not far from the later-day Trakehnen was named Gross Britannien (Great Britain), with Heinrichs Wolde (Henry's Wood) close by. Many Scots emigrated there and founded families. I think that William von Simpson the writer, whose family seat was at Georgenburg, must have belonged to an earlier Scottish family, for the name rings too much of the Highlands ever to have originated in Eastern Europe.

Rünger writes that after conquering the country the knights took over the breeding of the native horses, the 'Schweiken' as they were known. In the so-called farm studs, the native horse was bred apart from the heavier horse which the knights had brought with them. Heavy horses served as riding horses, and the lighter horse was used on the land—a position which is completely reversed in most European countries today, but was common form in medieval Europe, including England. In the year 1400, Rünger shows sixty-one studs belonging to the Order, and five ecclesiastical studs.

Very soon the Order learnt the value of these little East Prussian horses, which worked so hard and helped the country people. It was found that they could be used for light cavalry work and as pack ponies.

Of the sixty-one studs belonging to the Order most were built near their forts or headquarters, and near river bases, as in Marienburg, Danzig, Elbing, Königsberg, Balga,

Tapiau, Ragnit. And although the breeding of the heavier horses and the lighter type was kept strictly separate, the latter gradually came to be bred on heavier lines. The East Prussian horse was bred with the greatest care, and highly valued. At the time of the Order, and later, one good East Prussian horse equalled three good working bondmen.

It seems clear that blood from these studs went out into the Province, especially as landowners were bound to supply two light cavalrymen, when required to do so by the Order, and so they tried to breed horses for themselves instead of buying. Owing to the influence of the Order's studs, there was less disturbance in the land.

Unfortunately the period of knights and knightly chivalry came to an end; their power, which was generally in the western part of the Province diminished. With the disappearance of the knights, so with the many studs, and with horse-breeding generally. The heavy horse vanished almost completely, so that later only traces of the breed could be found in Ermland. But the Schweiken, the descendants of the wild horse came again into their own.

Now the country was devastated by the plague and by 1709 the country was terribly depopulated. Both the remaining population and horse-breeding were in a very sad condition.

It was through the foresight of King Frederick William I that new life came into East Prussia. On the advice of Prince Leopold von Anhalt-Dessau the heavy swamp land, from which the plague had taken its toll of the inhabitants, between Gumbinnen and Ebenrode and which belonged to the State, was taken over. The Pissa Canal was built, and other water-works put in hand. Owing to the shortage of labour, 300 soldiers from Memel were brought in and in six years, 10,600 acres of good arable land were reclaimed. Out

26

of this land, with two other estates added—Willkumlauken and Jodszlauken—Trakehnen was founded in 1732.

All the available stud material from outlying studs and breeding centres: Sperling, Beatricken, Insterburg, Budoponen, Gudden, Ragnit and Schreitlauken was collected and sent to Trakehnen. Studs in West Prussia had already been given up in 1717 and replaced by herds of cattle. Altogether in the Royal Trakehnen Stud, 1,101 horses, including 513 mares, were gathered at Frederick William's command. The horses were very uneven in type—and may have included specimens of the remainder of the heavy breed, which the Order had formerly bred in these studs.

The new stud was under the direction of a stud manager and a bailiff who worked entirely separately and each had to give a special account of himself to the king. Unfortunately in this new enterprise the king was sadly disappointed, first, because he had over-estimated the profit which the farm lands and the stud would bring in, and secondly, because his severity and displeasure were greatly feared by his subordinates and this subsequently led to dishonesty. Trakehnen had been built with the intention of being a financial help to the state exchequer, but this was not fulfilled, and the stud itself made very little progress.

In 1739 the king gave the whole property to the crown prince (later Frederick the Great). Luckily for Trakehnen, President von Dombardt who lived in Gumbinnen, took over the supreme direction of the stud and it was run on orderly lines. It was ordained that the stud was to supply horses to the royal stables and everything was done to even out and to improve the material. Good breeding stock was, however, extremely difficult to find.

Herr von Burgsdorf, a later director of the stud and one of its principal improvers, writes that in the summer of

1742 Frederick the Great sent from a stud in Bohemia, which he had captured—probably from Prince Dietrich-stein—36 stallions, 138 mares and 107 young horses. These were mainly Neapolitan, big, long necked, with such big heads and Roman noses that they were unable to eat out of ordinary mangers, and their hindquarters were very weak. In May 1746 the king gave the stud three Bohemian stallions: Prälat, Dietrichsteiner and Kuperwitzer, which were no better than the earlier horses.

Stallions from many countries were used apparently without any special aim. It is said that the 356 stallions which were used in Trakehnen, whilst the stud was in royal private ownership between 1732 and 1786, a period of fifty-four years, included the following breeds:

Trakehner breed	185
Without any pedigree	36
Prussian bred	31
English	15
Rosenburger	14
Danish	10
Turk	10
From Berlin without pedigree	5
Spanish	3
Neapolitan	2
Oriental	1
Persian	1
Barb	1
Egyptian	1
Bulgarian	1
Schlesian	1
Animals from Bohemia, of no great value and little used	39
	356

The Danish horses probably came from the Fredericks-borger Stud, and if so were very well bred, from Spanish (Andalusian) and Neapolitan lines. They were of very elegant conformation, and possessed a lively but nice temperament, a strong stride and high action. These animals were very highly regarded by all who valued horses. The Fredericksborger Stud existed from 1650 to 1839. At one time Denmark played almost the chief role in Europe in the breeding of good horses.

It is clear that horses in Trakehnen were bred in a very amateur and haphazard way, at that time probably no one thought of establishing one particular breed, and of the horses bred, not always the best were kept, for these were sold away for economical reasons. But during the next 150 years East Prussia supplied horses to the army.

On the death of King Frederick the Great the stud went out of royal private ownership, and became the property of the Prussian State, and from that time on a proper breeding programme was planned and organised. The mares were selected for conformation and suitable blood lines, any which did not fulfil a certain standard was sorted out and sold. Many had not enough bone, were ewe-hocked and had bent hind legs and several other faults. By today's standards they were also on the small side—roughly 15hh. The smallest was registered as only 14.1hh, and the biggest who must have looked like a giantess to her stable companions, 16.1hh. It is clear that at this time these horses must have been comparatively small and light, later they became much heavier and had more bone. But again after World War I, a lighter more versatile and elegant horse was to be required.

Those mares which were retained were sorted out into two groups: riding and carriage horses; and into five herds for colour: black, brown, chestnut, and two mixed herds.

29

The three single-colour herds belonged to the carriage horses, mixed colours to riding horses. The lighter type of mares were kept in Trakehnen and the heavy type in Bajohrgallen.

For the next 150 years many were the qualities required of the Trakehner horse: conformation, temperament, stamina, easy feeding, ability to cross a country or to pull a carriage at the trot for hours on end, and, equally important, to work in the fields at every type of agricultural work. From now on Trakehnen had not the single purpose to supply horses for the royal stables, but had to provide stallions to stand in the various districts and so help the farmers and small landowners to improve the breed of the native East Prussian working mares. Eventually several hundred of the best stallions were to be found standing in all country districts. Four of the most north-easterly studs were called 'Lithuanian Land Studs' and came under the stud director of Prussia–Lithuania.

From the year 1787 all horses born in Trakehnen were branded on the off-thigh with the single seven-pointed elk-

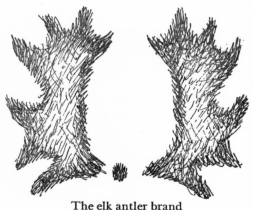

The elk antler brand

antler brand. From 1888 the ordinary East Prussian horse was branded with double antler brand on the near thigh.

Apart from horse-breeding there was also a mule stud in Trakehnen. The following rather remarkable genetic crossings were also ordered, and had to be carried out by the Stud Director, Count Lindenau, during a period of six years: crossing of a bull with a mare and a she-donkey, of horse and donkey stallions with cows, whereby it was hoped to raise an extraordinary animal called the Jumarron, of which a specimen is supposed to have been shown in the menagerie in Cassel. Luckily these odd experiments in no way detracted from the proper programme of breeding.

In the summer of 1794 a corps of Polish insurgents neared the frontier and threatened to overrun East Prussia, and so the stud had to move further inland, but as soon as the trouble was over, it returned once more to Trakehnen. After the lost battle of Jena and Auerstadt in October 1806 the Neustadt stud was completely overrun and Trakehnen had to be evacuated across the Memel towards Schaulen in Lithuania, and returned a year later. Those horses which were left behind, fell into French hands after Blücher's capitulation, and in addition Trakehnen had to give up some of the best mares from the riding herd and two of the best stallions. But both the stud and the mule stud were much depleted, and most of Count Lindenau's work undone.

In 1812 Trakehnen again had to be evacuated, and this was a much more serious and difficult matter. Herr von Burgsdorff says in his letters that he as director was ordered to take 203 stallions and 581 stud mares towards Marienwerder, Landsberg and on to Ohlau and Neisse. After the battle of Bautzen—Napoleon's victory over the Russians and Prussians—they were taken to Krzyanowitz, between

31

Ratibor and Troppau. There, overlooked by the Carpathians, they had to spend the whole summer, and not before September 1813 could they return homewards via Tschenstochau, Lowicz, Plock, Soldau and Rastenburg. This exercise in moving well-bred horses in herds over a distance of hundreds of kilometres is almost incredible, with the difficulties of the journey there in over two feet of snow, the weak ice-covering over the Vistula, the thaw, provision of fodder, the war, and then the return journey through a divided Poland.

Herr von Burgsdorff was probably one of the most noteworthy of the directors of Trakehnen, for he was responsible for this evacuation of the stud before the invasion of Napoleon's army. Needless to say Napoleon was quite anxious to get hold of some of these horses.

Von Burgsdorff describes that year 1812–13 in a letter to Count Karl Lehndorff-Steinort, the founder of the East Prussian cavalry regiment. He refers to a letter received from Count Lehndorff in which the latter hoped to buy some mares at the next sale:

'I only returned with the main part of the stud from Upper Silesia, through Poland on October 8th and therefore our sale has had to be postponed until the spring. If, by then, my dear friend, you have not found what you require I will do my best for you. Around twenty distinguished five-year-old mares will certainly come up for sale but the best of them will fetch high prices as riding horses, and the not so good are not suitable for you . . .'

Von Burgsdorff then bitterly regrets that he has had to be occupied with such trivial affairs, whilst Lehndorff was away fighting:

'In the preceding winter we were ordered to flee, the head stud-master, old Below, with the stallions was sent to Pomerania, and I with 581 stud horses, first to Neumark then to Upper Silesia, where the stud-master followed. You will know about this and also of my affection and worry over my charges, as well as how deeply the privation and hardship of such a march affected me. Considering the weather and the dreadful conditions of every sort, there were tremendous difficulties in moving such a large number of animals, and to see to everything attendant on them.

'Still, we have come through, and I am, myself, astonished at our luck. We only lost one $2\frac{1}{2}$ year-old from a broken leg. None of the horses was ill and my stallions have come through as if they had remained at home the whole time. Only 14 foals were lost in foaling out of 180 mares during the period of service 1812 to foaling 1813—very few considering the dreadfully tiring marches and continual changes of food.

'In Bischwitz not far from Strehlen we got the mares into quarters; 161 $3\frac{1}{2}$ and $2\frac{1}{2}$ year-old mares were quartered beyond Grottkau and just as many young stallions found quarters in the neighbourhood of Neustadt. I needed all my strength to cope with this dislocation and to be in all the places where it was necessary for me to be, but the massing of our troops in Silesia left no place where I could keep all the horses together. The foaling season was better than I had hoped, the foals were strong, as I had fed the mares well. The service season was in full swing, when, because of the Battle of Bautzen, we had to move on.

'With heavily in-foal mares, quite young foals, some of which were born on the march, I then moved further towards the Bohemian border and became involved in dreadful columns of refugees. My feeling and my pain over all

33

that was happening and my own unhappiness is not to be described. Thank God, it is now only a dream. Near Troppau we halted, and the armistice allowed us to draw breath. After 14 days interruption the stallion service began again. The foaling had ended, everything remained sound and even in the wet weather in good condition.

'On the 8. 9. with Russian passports I began our return march through Poland—luckily I found a fodder store and I was not ashamed to give each mare 12lb of oats, 10lb of hay and a bundle of straw. I had to keep their strength up, for there were long marches in mud, rain and cold weather, and nights spent under the open sky—which necessitated giving them more than they would have got in peaceful Trakehnen. Very often my tent was put up in a market place in the middle of Russian troops. There I had a big bed made up with hay, and the oats were also taken from God's good earth! Once only did I share a stable with the mares near the Moravian border, the stallions usually had boxes—which we often had first to build! Without any losses we arrived here and everyone found the horses in good condition.

'Up to now I have only lost four foals in down-foaling which is really fortunate and alone worth a lot to the King. All my people have groomed and cared for the animals in the best possible way, and never, never can I repay them for their love and obedience, they and I have lost weight and we have suffered greatly. One of the best has already died, and with your friend it quite recently stood between Debit and Credit, but I hope now I have pulled through and my people too. Even when I tell myself sometimes "you were not ineffective" I still realise that we have done nothing to compare with our brave soldiers.

'Previously I had asked for my recall, I wanted to go in

Page 35 The inner courtyard of the Marienburg. It needs little imagination to picture the knights of 600 years ago watering their horses at the well

Page 36 (above) All that remains of the Marienburg which covered six acres of land. The once-busy river Nogat is in the foreground; *(below)* part of the hand-painted dinner service presented to the Director of Trakehnen, Herr von Burgsdorff

the field—but I was ordered to remain at my post and I had to obey. My wife's ill-health made it necessary for her to take the baths, and as she needed a second cure, I had to decide to return alone and leave her with her sister-in-law Frau von Normann in Silesia. Pray God, she will return much strengthened in the summer. You can imagine how sad and lonely I have been all this winter. Days when the post comes are a holiday for me and my recuperation the care and observation of my beloved animals...'

The Province of East Prussia, which included the 500 breeders, showed its gratitude to Herr von Burgsdorff by the presentation of a very beautiful dinner service, whose principal ornament was a 2ft high hand-painted vase, on the one side a view of Trakehnen and on the other a painting of Cryer, an English Thoroughbred stallion. Real gold was used for further decoration. Included in the service were eighteen heavily gilded plates, from the royal Prussian porcelain factory at Berlin, each with a painting by the master Litfas of stallions standing in Trakehnen, of whom Herr von Burgsdorff was particularly fond. Sometimes the background was of East Prussian scenery, or an elk, a bison or Trakehner motifs. On one of the plates is a painting of Nedjed, a grey Arab which the director found in the London streets, in a cab and in not very good condition. Nedjed (Poisoned Arrow) was brought to Trakehnen and stood there for twelve years, he became one of the most famous sires.

Later, also in recognition of his services, Lithuania presented Herr von Burgsdorff with a beautifully wrought silver cup—on the lid three galloping horses, and round the cup beautiful reproductions of stallions.

The rescue of the dinner service some 140 years later

37

C

after World War II, by a great-great-niece of Herr von Burgsdorff, is in itself a story of remarkable courage and achievement, and an epic in the history of the Province.

Slowly the number of Trakehnen bred stallions increased and some English Thoroughbred and half-breds were imported; Bohemian stallions were no longer used, and other breeds variously decreased in numbers. Herr von Burgsdorff had used several excellent Arab stallions which included Nedjed and Bagdadly, and English half-bred stallions Pretender, Driver and Reprobate. This gives some idea of the further development of the East Prussian and Trakehnen breed of horses. There are several good books written on the actual breeding of this time and I do not propose to go further except to mention the Thoroughbred stallion Perfectionist, born in England in 1899, by Persimmon out of Perfect Dream.

Although Perfectionist only stood three years in Trakehnen he probably had the greatest influence, on the subsequent breed of horses, of any other sire at any time in the whole history of the development of this particular breed. Unfortunately through an accident in his box he had to be destroyed. But in his three years at stud he got 131 foals, and from these 32 stallions and 37 brood mares were kept. Eventually, through three or four of his sons, there were 156 stallions at stud and 293 brood mares.

It seems that some people did not approve of so much 'blood' for Director von Oettingen said later: 'I am certain that in the last 40 years, we have had one Thoroughbred stallion, of whom the greatest enemy of Thoroughbred blood must agree, that Trakehnen never saw the like before; this was Persimmon's son Perfectionist.' Persimmon was by St Simon. His grandson was the famous Tempelhüter—all four horses were dark brown. In 1910 von Oettingen founded the drag-hunt and 1911 saw the first cross-country race in Trakehnen.

In the summer of 1914, as war broke out, Trakehnen had to be evacuated for the fourth time. Six hundred of the most valuable horses were transported to Graditz and Neustadt, and as these studs were too small, three grassland farms in the Riesengebirge and an unoccupied Thoroughbred stud near Düren in the Rheinland were hired. By 18 August Trakehnen was completely emptied.

Count Sponeck, who was then director describes the evacuation:

'A refugee column of 1,850 people, 462 stud horses, 260 working horses, 650 cattle, 250 working oxen, and 313 bullocks left early on the 18th because of the nearness of the Russians to Trakehnen (this time the Russians were no longer allies). Those who read this list, cannot imagine what it was like on the roads as the hundreds of thousands of refugees moved slowly forwards. Only those who experienced it can know what an amount of foresight, energy and authority it required to keep such a column together, and it was due to Steward Conradi who led the trek, that they came through all difficulties in a remarkable way and arrived at their destination.'

Imagine trying to keep together a column of nearly 2,000 people, through thick and thin in the midst of war, armies, refugees, and the slow-moving herds of cattle, oxen, and waggons; and the organisation required to arrange food and shelter at night for all these people and animals in already overcrowded villages. It must have been a gigantic task.

The stud returned to Trakehnen in 1919, after the damage to eighty-three buildings had been repaired and the rest of the devastation had been cleared up. As one can imagine a lot of rebuilding had to be done, both to the premises, and to the breed of horses. No longer was the lighter type of cavalry or remount horse required, since the Treaty of Versailles had abolished the army, and therefore this outlet ceased entirely.

CHAPTER THREE

The Object of Breeding

IN 1922 Count Siegfried Lehndorff took over the director-ship of the stud in Trakehnen, and realised that it was now necessary to breed a heavier type of horse, which could be used more and more on the land. This conception of a 'heavier' horse must not be confused with our British heavy horses, Suffolks, Clydesdales etc, which are a cold-blood breed, particularly suited to the heavy clay soil in many parts of England. Probably most of the land in East Prussia was medium soil, and around Trakehnen we know that it was taken from swamp land. Other studs supplied heavier stallions, mainly Oldenburger, which were put to the East Prussian mares, and so where necessary produced a working-horse type. But Trakehnen remained true to its ideals, the improvement of the East Prussian through the Thorough-bred—but on heavier lines, so that a good sort of blood heavyweight hunter type began to appear.

It was an enormously difficult task, since the heavier sort of Thoroughbred stallion with plenty of bone is almost non-existent. However, the mares were carefully weeded out, future sires selected from the young colts with great care, and horses were bred with more substance and bone than heretofore.

41

The changing times brought with them a new sport—dressage and show jumping opened the gate to a new and vital interest and riders demanded horses which could compete in the show ring. All the young horses in training took part in the drag-hunts over obstacles with which we in Britain have become acquainted through our Olympic Horse Trials. At the same time racing for warm-blood horses became quite popular. In all these sports the Trakehner horse showed unusual promise and ability, and a great number of them were sold annually. Figures given show that in 1936 there were 1,289 stallions in East Prussia; 89,628 mares were covered, and in 1938–9 horses numbered 478,499. A surplus of 32,800 horses were *annually* sold away from the country. These figures are for cold- and warm-blood horses. This strikes one as an astounding number, but it does show how the whole Province was devoted to breeding horses.

Perhaps it is interesting to go even further into the sales and see which foreign countries were most interested in acquiring Trakehner horses and for what purposes they were needed.

Europe

Bulgaria	Stud and working horses
Czechoslovakia	Show horses, remounts, stallions
England	Dressage horses for the circus
Finland	Riding and working horses
France	Riding horses
Holland	Riding and show horses
Hungary	Show horses
Italy	Breeding stallions and riding horses
Lapland	Stud and working horses
Lithuania	Brood mares and stallions
Luxemburg	Working horses

Europe (continued)

Poland	Stallions and working horses
Roumania	Stud and working horses
Russia	About 5,000 riding and working horses and 300 brood mares and stallions
Spain	Mares and stallions
Sweden	Riding and working horses and stallions
Switzerland	Show and working horses and brood mares

North and South America

Brazil	Brood mares and stallions
Canada (since 1946)	Brood mares and stallions
Columbia	Stallions for remount studs
Mexico	Stallions
USA	Stallions for remount studs, show horses

Africa and Far East

Africa, East	Stud horses
Africa, South West	Working and stud horses
India	Working and stud horses
Japan	Working horses

There seem to be few countries in the world untrodden by the Trakehner horses; but strangely England seems to be one of the few 'horsy' countries which failed to recognise the great potentialities of these horses. Since the war probably some have found their way to our shores as it is said that the Life Guards had some horses with the elk brand in their ranks.

All Trakehner horses which had been earmarked for stud purposes had to undergo a year's training and finally,

43

a quite thorough test. It was the accepted belief that horses which were destined to carry on the race must prove that they would be worthy parents, and it shows a very common-sense attitude. During training they were ridden in the school, and driven in trotting waggons. In autumn when the weather allowed the young entires were ridden across country and it was obvious that the most important part of their education lay in the Trakehnen hunt country.

The testing of the stallions used to take place in Zwion near Georgenburg. At the age of $2\frac{1}{2}$, every young horse which had been reserved by his owner as a possible sire had to go to Zwion in the autumn and there the young entire, under his rider, underwent a 3-day cross-country test; on the first day 10km, second day 10km, and on the third day 13km with a speed gallop of 3km. On each day there were 10 fences to be jumped. The time allowed, and in which this whole distance must be done, was 4min per kilometre, but even this speed was only on the grounds that it would give the young horse time for a refusal and therefore he would not be disqualified unnecessarily, since enough time remained for him to take the obstacle again. Generally the horses were able to do the kilometre in 3min and pulled up fresh and with clean legs. At first sight this test sounds quite easy but we must remember that the entires were only $3\frac{1}{2}$ years old.

The whole work leading up to the test had to be correctly and easily followed up in the test itself and experience showed that this was possible without detracting from the young horse's stamina. On the other hand the director of the examining establishment obtained during the year's training and education a clear picture of the young stallion's complete possibilities and potentialities: his health, action, temperament, appetite and energy. In forming a

44

final opinion of a stallion, the experience which he had gained throughout his education, and not entirely the result of the test—which most of them completed successfully—was taken carefully into consideration, and decided the director in his final choice of suitable entries for the Stud Book.

The stallions obtained marks for their cross-country, and also for their action in the walk, trot and gallop, which usually took place a few days before the performance under the rider. On the day of the cross-country test there was always another veterinary examination for soundness.

As one might expect those entires with more Thorough-bred blood did better, but the test was also the best method for discovering which of the stallions with little 'blood' failed in energy and hardness. Roughly 10 per cent failed to pass, but the object of the test was not to find out the most excellent qualities which a horse could possess but to weed out those which failed, in some direction, to come up to standard. When one realises that the candidates which appeared for training and testing had already undergone a thorough inspection by six or seven different people—such as the director of breeding, the chief stud director, the Trakehnen stud director, the stud-master of his home stud, the director of the Stud Book Society, and the breeder of the stallion himself, it shows that the training and final test with a 10 per cent failure to pass was a really thorough and severe weeding-out of potential stallions.

The testing of the mares followed other lines, because no farmer, smallholder or peasant could afford to keep a mare purely for the purpose of breeding. However well-bred she might be, she carried out her share of farm work, sometimes in foal and sometimes with her foal also trotting along beside her. (When I was in East Prussia some eight

45

years ago it was no uncommon sight to see fifteen or sixteen mares working on a 50 acre field, with a dozen foals walking, cantering around or asleep by the roadside). Every day the East Prussian mare carried out a 'test' in the work which she performed for her owner, for any mare who was unable to work, either because of temperament or because she was a difficult feeder was sooner or later sold.

The authorities thought that it was necessary to go to some trouble to arrange a sensible test for the mares, but it was sometime before a worthwhile test was arrived at. Soon after World War I, in East Prussia, 3 year-old mares were tested at the walk, trot and canter, but nothing much was achieved owing to the different capabilities of the riders, who were mostly farmers' sons. The mares were then tested for their performances in pulling heavy loads over distances. Two 18 year-old brood mares carried out a test over 45km of good roads with hills, pulling a 3 ton load. They completed the distance in 252min, which equals 5min 36sec per km!

But this method of testing was not entirely satisfactory because East Prussian mares are needed for many other purposes and qualities and since 1936, at the request of the small breeders, and according to experience gained in Pomerania and Mecklenburg, a test was arranged and took place in three phases:

1 Capabilities in ploughing: pairs, one coulter plough, working time 4hr, resistance of weight per horse 120kg, furrow width 30-35cm. Acreage under normal conditions 2.2 acres.

2 Performance: pairs, pulling heavy loads on even roads over 25km with $2\frac{1}{2}$ tons load, with waggon but not driver. The first 21km walk and trot as required, but not to exceed 6min per km. The last

46

4km walk not to exceed 11min per km.

3 Final test under riders: free walk, free trot without restriction. Gallop over 2km in 5min 30sec.

Between performance 1 and 2 a pause of 2hr; between 2 and 3 a pause of ½hr. All the tests took place on the same day. The mares had to be registered in the East Prussian Stud Book and had to carry a certificate that they had been covered.

The breeding target, that is to say the sort of horse which breeders were encouraged to aim for, should be an animal of exceptional qualities. Count Siegfried Lehndorff in *Ein Leben mit Pferden* gave the following desirable characteristics:

The brood mare should be middle-sized—about 16hh with roomy frame, short-legged, deep-chest, strong rump, forceful calibre, but withal a noble outlook, long, even, balanced strides, good nerve, with a quiet, willing-to-work temperament, and a hard and healthy constitution.

The stallion, as the representative of masculinity, must be overall of more consequence than the mare.

The result of these all-round ride and drive horses, was that they were solidly built, not too short in the back, medium bone, good deep girth with round full ribs. Especial emphasis was laid on the horse's temperament, and for riding purposes he had to have all-round good conformation. Small, noble heads are an ornament to any horse, and the way the head is carried shows courage and energy. The neck should be well-set and of the proper length, the withers properly formed. A ewe-neck was no more required than a bull-neck. The position and length of the shoulder had been improved throughout the years. The croup had, if possible, to be long, massive, well-muscled, and with a nice roundness. The deep round rump had to be of a marked depth. Balance and length of stride was always of importance, together with a light, airy trot—for the grace of the trot is remarkable to this breed. One could always be sure of a good strong gallop because there was sufficient of the English Thoroughbred blood in the breed to ensure it.

A horse of such conformation, with a quiet temperament, faultless, easily fed, quick and with staying power could just as well be used for farm work as for riding purposes.

Anyone interested in breeding will realise that to produce a worthwhile breed of horses much attention should be paid to the qualities of the mare who has as great, and possibly greater, influence upon her offspring as the sire. This truth has always been recognised by the Arabs; and it was also realised by the later directors of Trakehnen, for the East Prussian horse has acquired his superlative qualities as much through his dam's line as through that of his sire. And as if to acknowledge this fact the horses take their names from the first letter of the dam's name. The Thoroughbred stallion born in England in 1899, Perfectionist, was out of Perfect Dream; his son the famous Tempelhüter (1905) was out of Teichrose, and this continues so throughout the table of pedigrees.

It is of the greatest importance to possess a thorough understanding of the rearing and growth of young horses. Those who had the responsibility for the breeding and rearing of Trakehner and East Prussian horses knew well that the first year of growth is of the greatest consequence, and that it is then that the foundation for better or worse is laid. Lack of attention at this time is too obvious, and even

48

with care and intensive feeding will never be repaired later on. One might really say that the first *two* years of life are of the most importance, this includes the foal's first twelve months on this earth and the eleven months previously before he appeared!

The Trakehner takes about the same time to mature as other warm-blood breeds and after the third full year the greater part of his growth is ended and the young horse can be used with understanding and without damage. It was for this reason that the training of the young entires at Zwion began at 2½ years old. The fourth and fifth years are needed for the horse to make up in proportion, ie the depth of girth, rump and breast, and the whole filling-out of the animal. At five years it seems that further growth is impossible, and the horse reaches his peak at 7 or 8 years of age. The length of his complete capabilities usually lasts until 20 years. The average height of these horses is 16.1hh.

To understand the development of a half or warm-blood breed of horses, one should be *au fait* with Thoroughbred breeding. The family tree of the East Prussian and the Trakehner horse contains a great infusion of both Thoroughbred and Arab blood and in fact every horse registered in the Stud Book can trace his ancestry back, often through Eclipse, to the Darley and Godolphin Arabians and the Byerley Turk. When one remembers that originally in 1732 only the best of the native horses of East Prussia were used as brood mares—and that this breed is now about 260 years old, having been continually improved for generations by careful selection, rearing and training —it is not to be wondered that before the war the East Prussian was known throughout the world for his versatility.

It is noteworthy that more often than not the stallion

49

whose conformation, performance and character were of the best, reproduced himself exactly in his sons, and also very often in his daughters. This is one of the most important hereditary characteristics of a top-class stallion.

Herr von Oettingen, at one time Director of Trakehnen did some very deep thinking upon the subject of breeding. We have a clear picture of the care and thought which this highly specialised expert devoted to the constant improvement of the breed. Here are two very worthwhile observations of his:

Eliminate all unnecessary influence or characteristics. Never use a mare or stallion which shows some really unwanted peculiarity.

Bad feeding or good feeding can change the stamp or type; as can climate, soil and the way the horse is kept.

Herr von Oettingen further finds that the primary inherited factors are health; strength; hardness; action; stamina; habits; and, from use, the construction of the bones, for example the strong hocks of the hackney, the straight strong shoulders of the cart-horse, the light frame of the sprinter, and so on. From frequent and early practice in galloping of the Thoroughbred, the previously bent hind leg has become straighter, and a previously slight wither has developed into a prominent one.

The offspring of horses which have been driven, have proved easier to train to drive than the offspring of horses which have never been driven. And exactly the same applies to our present-day show jumpers. A breed loses its value, if for several succeeding generations, nothing is expected of it; for example, if the animals are neither

50

trained, worked, used, raced, etc. Finally the only heritable potential would be weakness, lack of stamina and other faults.

He goes on to say that one should breed from parents with natural tendencies, talents and abilities if one requires the same ability in the offspring, and there are many examples in Thoroughbred breeding of inherited talents, from Eclipse onwards. The belief in especial inherited tendencies and abilities is the chief stimulus for a breeder to carry out diligent and calculated work. Without such firm belief there would be a great danger of negligence in breeding. The greatest pleasure of the breeder would go if he did not heed the most interesting part, namely, the inheritance of natural tendencies, and this would cause a lowering of every standard.

Herr von Oettingen also observes that inheritance in horse breeding is the more constant, the higher the percentage of well-bred ancestors in the pedigrees of both parents. And his definition of 'well-bred' has not the implication we mean when we think of thoroughbred. For the infusion of Thoroughbred in a well-bred Shetland pony, for example, is the last thing a Shetland pony breeder requires. Well-bred means the desired potentialities, tendencies, and abilities and talents which we require in any special given breed. Therefore the more numerous the appearance of 'well-bred' characteristics in a horse's pedigree, the greater his own potentiality.

It is clear then that the crossing between a Thoroughbred or Arab and a cold-blood horse, may have the effect of producing a horse for an especial purpose, but it is not suitable or desirable to breed further from this product. In my experience, one would then be breeding the bad or least desirable qualities from both parents; bad qualities are more easily reproduced than good ones.

What can be inherited? Almost anything: unbelievable trifles and nuances in conformation, action and temperament; the physical proportions of any part of the body and also length of hair, texture, hair twirls; courage; fear; naughtiness and trust; bad and good fertility; immunity to certain illnesses; long life; good and bad habits. But the so-called hereditary defects such as blindness, spavin, crib-biting, roaring, broken wind, etc, are less often inherited, and quite often not at all.

Spavin is an inflammation of the tissues caused by the jarring of badly set-on bones, or bad conformation. This causes a thickness. The inflammation is obviously not inherited, but the bad conformation is, and this subsequently leads to jarring, therefore one should consider carefully before breeding from horses with bad conformation. An exception to this rule was Percival who, because of noticeable spavin was cast from Trakehnen, and taken into the private stud of Herr von Simpson. He subsequently got 200 remounts, 50 stud mares and 25 stallions, not one of whom showed the slightest sign of spavin, nor did in succeeding generations. There are many other examples.

As far as crib-biting, air-swallowing, etc, are concerned, usually only really tough horses show this habit and it is only about five per cent inherited; it is almost always caused by energetic horses being insufficiently worked. It is only when animals are chronically ill, and their whole physical condition is disturbed by the habit, that they are obviously unsuited as parents. Ormonde was a roarer, and Gallinule too, and as far as it is known neither passed on the tendency.

But constitutional weakness can be inherited and it is such weakness which may eventually lead to bad habits.

Page 53 (above) Persimmon by St Simon, owned by King Edward VII. Persimmon's son, Perfectionist, left 32 stallions and 37 brood mares at Trakehnen. Persimmon as a four-year-old; *(below)* a forest road in West Prussia leading towards the Frisches Haff

Page 54 (right) St Anthony and the baby Jesus, a statue of hope and mercy; *(below)* Gutstadt Church; a small market town which was almost destroyed in 1945

And since constitutional weakness can be inherited so can constitutional hardness, meaning robust health. These two factors hand-in-hand are of the utmost importance for stud animals. So one needs to eliminate weakness and encourage hardness, therefore one tries to breed only from strong, healthy animals.

Long legs, too short legs and bad temper are bad faults to breed from. Also mares who are bad feeders, when there is no obvious reason for it, as it is presumed that they will not be able to feed their foals. Mares running to fat are also bad mothers. These two latter faults in the stallion must be noted but are not so important in him as in a mare.

Every director of Trakehnen stressed the point that much careful thought must be given to a mating, not any stallion with any mare, but the *right* stallion considering the type of mare. One must be sure what sort of foal one wants, and not just hope for the best and that something useful will result. A certain weakness in the mare must be offset by the strength of the stallion: for example, nervousness in the mare must be offset by the calm, equable disposition of the stallion; a dull, slow mare must find a highly couraged stallion and vice versa. One must bear in mind when considering a pairing, not only the mare and stallion, but their parents and grand-parents. Also it must be decided if the desired foal is only to be used for working purposes or if the line is to be continued for stud purposes. For a long-term policy it is better that the same pairing continues.

Count Lehndorff, who was well-known at British Turf meetings both before World War I and afterwards when he took over as stud director of Trakehnen, had very similar ideas. It was during his management that racing for warm-blood horses became very popular in many parts of

55

D

Germany, and breeding plans had to be modified to meet this demand. It is, therefore, interesting to read in his book *Ein Leben mit Pferden* (A Life with Horses) his ideas on what was necessary to make a good racehorse.

Count Lehndorff's father wrote:

'A good racehorse must have first, health—second, health —and third, plenty of health and the idea of using Thoroughbred blood is to inject this health into the muscles, constitution and nerves of the entire warm-blood race.

'Naturally after proper training a racehorse's heart and lungs are not only more healthy but also sounder than those of an ordinary working horse, and it has been proved that a Thoroughbred in training has between 2 and 3 pints more blood, the lungs are capable of pumping more oxygen into the blood-stream, and the pulse therefore beats slower—about 30 (28.032) beats to the minute—so that it is capable of greater exertion and is not so easily tired. A normal horse's heart beats are 36-40 per minute.

'The Thoroughbred's heart is definitely bigger than that of a normal horse, whose heart weighs 8-9lb; with the former it is sometimes more than 13lb. The arteries and veins correspond to the size of the heart and after exertion, both by Thoroughbred horses and Arabs, the whole network can be seen under the skin. And because the circulation is able to do so much more, the result is a greater capacity for exertion. The better the circulation the better are the muscles and nerves fed, and the more easily is the used blood circulated back through the veins. Well fed muscles are able to work better. The bigger the heart, the more complete and healthy the circulatory system and the more energy in the horse, and therefore the greater endurance and speed.'

Lehndorff himself wrote:

'In East Prussia great worth was attached to conformation, for example, a Thoroughbred stamp—and vigour and
strength were overlooked. So that I was often over-ruled in
awarding premiums, when I wanted to give the premium
to a strong mare with perhaps less 'blood', rather than to
a blood-type riding mare who was scarcely stronger than a
medium Thoroughbred.

'Of the four German warm-blood breeds, the East Prussian has the most Thoroughbred blood, and therefore has
the most endurance but it is also the lightest type; the next
is the Hanoverian, the Holstein, and lastly the Oldenburger and East Friesian. These last have the least 'blood'
and are by far the stronger and heavier.

'There is often not enough information about the use of
Thoroughbred blood in a warm-blood breed. Usually one
should use a Thoroughbred stallion more for the breeding
of working or riding horses, than for stud purposes. But in
order to keep up the stamina and endurance of the warm-
blood breed from time to time use can be made of a Thoroughbred sire, but only a really good strong one because
there is always the danger that the breed will become too
light. But if I wanted to buy a useful all-round performer
I would give the vote to the produce of the Thoroughbred
stallion rather than to one whose Thoroughbred blood was
in the second or third ancestral line.'

It seems clear that Count Lehndorff was against the use
of much Thoroughbred blood for breeding purposes, except
now and again to improve the breed. When a warm-blood
breed such as the East Prussian exists, and has existed for a
long period of time, with its own typical characteristics, the

introduction of outside blood, be it Thoroughbred or Arab must be done most carefully. If not, the warm-blood characteristics would be lost and the breed would run to almost Thoroughbred type, which was clearly undesirable. The East Prussian is, I believe, the only *pure* warm-blood breed in Germany.

That is to say, the breed is free, or has been free for at least the last hundred years, from any other warm-blood strain—contrary to the Hanoverian or Holstein, which always have had recourse to 'outside' warm-blood. Both of these used Irish Draught Horse and Yorkshire Coach Horse in byegone days to maintain the characteristics of the breed and type. And perhaps this accounts for the differences of type in other warm-blood breeds, whereas my own researches and observations have shown me that the East Prussian and Trakehner, with few exceptions, are 'as like as peas in a pod'.

To revert to the actual testing of horses, both stallions and mares are tested today, but not as in Trakehnen, since the stallions are scattered over Western Germany and stand at the farms or studs from which they serve the mares in their districts. The mares are also scattered, working on their owners' farms or smallholdings and so no proper even tests can be made. More especially the western provinces of Germany each have their own methods and arrangements for testing mares and stallions of every breed. Therefore Holstein varies from Hanover, and Westphalia from Friesland. This is a pity, but at least there is a test of performance and an examination, so that the breed is kept, as far as possible, on the highest level.

CHAPTER FOUR

The Native Land of the Trakehner

UNFORTUNATELY BEFORE the war, I never went quite as far east as East Prussia. Since the war, I have been privileged to visit the southern half of the Province twice; but what I know of the countryside in pre-war years comes from talking to many people who once lived there, and from them one can have a very fair picture of that lovely lost homeland which surrounded the stud Trakehnen. There were great forests and lakes, vast rolling corn fields; small towns and fishing villages; parks and manor houses with courtyards and houses for the work people, church, smithy, wheelwright's shop, and distillery. Every manor house was self-contained, and the little village which composed its workers and tenants, a self-supporting unit, looking to the head of the estate, the master, for guidance and if necessary protection.

From the previous chapters it will be realised just how great a role Trakehnen played in the life of the Province; perhaps a description of that 'paradise for horses' will give a clearer picture. Trakehnen was inseparable from the picture of buildings, trees, pastures and horses. The winter in East Prussia was long, cold and snowy, and spring came late. When it did come, with the arrival of the stork, it appeared with surprising suddenness and in no time it was summer, hot and sunny. Everywhere there were trees spread out in their early untouched greenery and everything would shimmer. In the distance one could hear the cuckoo call. The charm of this distant, unforgotten land is clear in the voices of the people describing it—long avenues of trees, bordering dusty roads, post and rails guarding the paddocks and, an unusual sight even for Trakehnen, a black-cock in the grass in all his blue, black and white finery.

In East Prussia, where hospitality and culture abounded, there was scarcely a village or a town, as in England, which did not have an historical background, scarcely a family who lived in the country who were not breeding horses— horses which were to be known and recognised throughout the world. The East Prussians lived for their horses, and their main stud at Trakehnen was the Newmarket of the warm-blood horses. There in the paddocks were the year-lings (just as you may see at Newmarket) who were to win great races, future Olympic dressage winners, great sires who were to found lines in a score of foreign countries, and quiet tempered mares with old and famous blood lines. A paradise indeed for horses, and for horse-lovers from all over the world.

One can picture a day in the life of pre-war Trakehnen. It is a marvellous morning; and breakfast is waiting in the Hotel Elch; there is a wonderful aroma of coffee every-where. The melody of East Prussia, at first only a soft note of something precious, has begun. Its refrain comes again and again—the whinny of a mare, peacefully swishing tails, and black and brown and chestnut herds. At the moment all is in harmony.

Great trees and wide pastures, the clap of a stork on a

roof, a foal who sniffs inquisitively, a carriage-and-four harness a-jingle, lakes, the wide moors, the forests and the elk. But there can be a harsher tone: the distant howl of a wolf in winter, the cold plush of snow falling upon snow, a stampeding of hooves, the shrill neigh of a stallion, and soon there will be the sound of gunfire coming near and nearer —ever nearer. Such will be the song of East Prussia, soft and beautiful, earnest, hard and finally cruel, until life dissolves into a deathly hush, the disintegration of a country. But the day is yet sunny, the morning early and there is much to see in Trakehnen.

The house in which the director of the stud lives, stands back in a small park. Before the door on the grass, stands a life-size statue of the stallion Tempelhüter, the worthy son of Perfectionist by the English Thoroughbred Persimmon. In the park wall is an old stone engraved with a seven-pointed elk's antler, the brand carried on the off thigh by all horses born in Trakehnen.

The village, which is surrounded and divided by its thick birch hedges, is large and completely self-sufficient. There are over 3,000 people whose sole concern is to attend directly or indirectly to the horses, and farm the 14,000 acres of land, for which over 400 working horses are kept. There are 9 schools with 14 teachers, a doctor and a chemist. There are 9 outlying farms, some of which stable the yearlings, and the 2 and 3 year-olds. Trakehnen has its own riding school, both indoor and outdoor, where at 4 years old, the young horses are schooled before being sold.

There is a pack of hounds, small by English standards, which hunt a drag over uncompromising fences—one of the best-known obstacles at the Badminton Olympic Horse Trials is a post and rails known as the Trakehner—and variously wide and deep ditches which separate the boundaries. Probably there is no province in Germany which lends itself better for riding. Drag-hunting begins around July after hay-making with fairly short drags of about 1,500m, as the young horses become fitter the distance being increased, over about 10,000 acres of suitable country, mostly grassland. Marvellous going with a good, willing, well-mannered young horse under one. And at the end of the four-month season, the hounds are usually so fit the going is really fast.

A dusty road divides two large paddocks of 50 acres or more. On each side mares and foals are grazing guarded by a mounted groom, for all the grooms are mounted when on duty with the various herds. One will lead them home and another bring up the rear as daylight fades and mares and foals must return to the yards. The evenness of these mares is impressive; each one appears, but for colour, to be a replica of the other. Many have foals or are soon about to foal and often the offspring of one particular sire is clearly recognisable. The flies in East Prussia are a fearful menace, but many of the paddocks are almost treeless; trees encourage flies and so they are reduced to a minimum, and the horses are comparatively free from this pest.

Can one imagine a more peaceful scene upon which to rest the eyes than numbers of mares and foals quietly feeding on good and sufficient grass? Count Lehndorff, one of the studs most famous directors discovered the best grass for horses is *Poa pratensis*, which they seem to prefer to any other kind; on the other hand one of the most useless is *Scleranthus* which horses will only eat when it is very young. Besides the horses about 2,000 cows are also grazed on the pastures—since the stud's officials always own several apiece, and every landworker has at least one.

Right in the centre of the contentedly grazing mares is a

stork industriously searching for frogs which are numerous in these low-lying meadowlands. Storks are an amazing sight to anyone who has not seen them before. They really seem to be the clowns of the bird world, with their ungainly bodies and big awkward beaks, and their incessant clacking and clapping on the roof-tops where they build their enormous untidy nests of twigs, like guardsmen's busbies. Sometimes waggon-wheels are placed on purpose on a roof to encourage the storks to build; they are thought to bring luck to the courtyard and everyone likes to see them about.

Back in Trakehnen itself, we pass one of the several stallion paddocks: there are always several stallions at stud. Some paddocks have a high hedge or a wall, but even so the stallion is able to see over the top of it. He is allowed to view his kingdom! In his paddock is a pleasant 'garden house', with climbing creepers hanging from its walls and roof—a large round loose box. With a background of beautiful trees, the stallion can really enjoy his freedom.

But everywhere is pleasantly free. One can wander at will down the shady drives, look in at the smithy, admire the gardens, drive over the sandy roads past the paddocks, through the farmlands to one of the subsidiary studs— Mattischkehmen, Dansekehmen, Taukenischken, Bajohrgallen and Jonastal, home of the chestnut mares—or to Gurdzen to see the black herd and on to Kalpakin or Burgsdorffshof. In the fields, meadows and forests, where the cuckoo's call echoes and re-echoes over the heads of a herd of deer and a solitary elk, whose large grotesque head bears eight-pointed shovel shaped antlers, the afternoon shadows deepen. The melody of East Prussia is still soft and low. But clouds are gathering over the lovely Province, clouds summoned at the behest of politicians and which will darken many lives for many, many years to come.

CHAPTER FIVE

October 1944: The Flight to the West

BY OCTOBER 1944 the war had been going on for five years and steadily the days dragged on. The German army, which had been sent so far into the desolate endlessness of the Russian countryside had been decimated like Napoleon's army years before, until at last a tight circle had been drawn around the lovely province of East Prussia. Steadily the remnants of the best regiments fought at terrific odds to save their homeland, and just as steadily brave men were crushed by relentless numbers, as the tide of war swept over the land. The army begged that the Province should be evacuated to the West, but Nazi Gauleiter Koch turned every plea and argument down. Hitler had said if Germany could not win then it could go under, and so no plans at all were made to avert the terrible tragedy which approached so mercilessly, encouraged by the very government which should have prevented it.

There was no planned evacuation, and no plans of any sort to save the population which then consisted of old men, women and children. No arrangements were made to allow the valuable stud at Trakehnen to be sent away to some place of safety. Until the very last moment nothing was done to get the horses out of the battle area, although the director Dr Ehlert had repeatedly gone to Koch to get permission to move his horses. When at last the permission came it was almost too late. In the meantime on his own initiative Dr Ehlert had sent some 250 stallions and foals away by rail.

The official order to evacuate came through in the early hours of 17 October, for on the previous day a great battle had begun and gunfire could be seen and heard at no great distance away. Everything was to be cleared out in two or three hours. About 1,200 horses had to be moved, but all the able-bodied grooms had been ordered to the home guard in a senseless attempt at defence, and only very old retired men and young boys were available to help with the 17 stallions and 370 brood mares. In spite of the almost overwhelming impossibility of getting the horses away at this late hour, incredible efforts were made, and the animals divided into ten herds, each herd being allocated three mounted grooms. They had nearly 70km to go to their first stopping place.

And so in October 1944 after over 200 years, the final evacuation took place and the last horses left Trakehnen. The dust raised by their departing hooves and which covered their exit from their paradise, settled down a few days later on a ruined and desolated stud. Gunfire and bombs destroyed what had taken generations of thought, hope and care to build.

The fleeing herds had to be kept going at the trot, otherwise the three mounted grooms would never have been able to keep the horses together. In a remarkable way they escaped the attentions of low-flying aircraft. Gumbinnen, an outlying village where some horses had been quartered

65

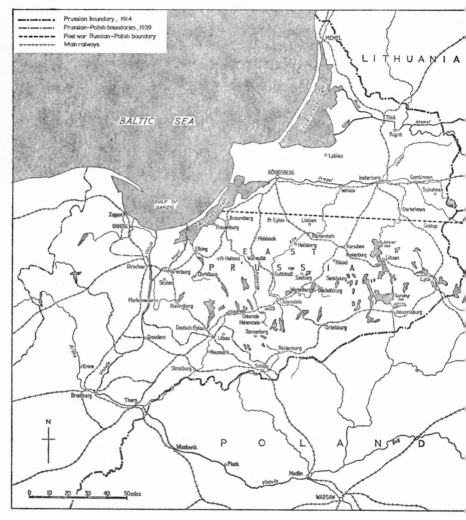

Map of East Prussia

66

and now a blazing ruin, caused a detour of several miles; treks of people and waggons were bypassed as the horses pushed relentlessly on their way, and in spite of every obstacle they arrived in Georgenburg at 6.30 that same evening. When the herds had been checked, not one horse or foal was missing or lame. And most of the horses were unshod!

Some horses were sent on by rail from Georgenburg across the Oder to the Graditz Stud near Torgau, to Neustadt an der Dosse or to Perlin near Schwerin. Those horses which were already evacuated to Mecklenburg had to conform to the Yalta Agreement, and, as they were the property of the German State, were handed over to the Russians. One of England's best-known horsemen, Brigadier Bolten, successfully managed to arrange for the rescue of twenty-eight mares by sending them across the Elbe where they were then distributed to various farms and estates until arrangements could be made for them all to go to Wiemerskamp near Hamburg.

This is but a poor description of the last days of Trakehnen and the collapse of the Province. In time perhaps an abler hand than mine will bring these historic days into the proper perspective of world history; but the time for that may not yet be ripe, for less than thirty years have elapsed. The sadness and the horror are still with us, and many people even now are homeless out of over 16 million who left eastern Europe and tried to start again in the West. They are still homeless because they cannot return to the land of their birth—as homeless as they were in the winter of 1944–5 when they turned their backs on all that was dear and familiar, and started on that long journey to the West, with nothing but their memories and their courage and their horses to accompany them.

To understand the situation better, it should be known that the evacuation of East Prussia, when it was finally allowed, was in two stages. In the middle of October 1944, the eastern frontier near Tilsit, Ragnit, Schlossburg, Ebenrode, Gumbinnen, Insterburg, Goldap and Trenburg was cleared, the inhabitants being sent to the west of the Province. Once the Russians were beaten, it was said, the people were to return to their own villages, and at once continue with their harvesting or sowing winter corn. But the Soviet army broke through in the middle of January 1945, and the great flight from the enemy of the whole Province took place. The stream of refugees grew rapidly, and the bridges over the rivers and the main roads were overcrowded, and quite often impassable.

On 22 January, Soviet tanks got through to Elbing and they rapidly threw a ring round the whole Province. The only way out was over the Pillauer Tief and then, if possible, over the small strip of land that was the Frische Nehrung. This passage over Pillau could hardly be used, as the German army, which had priority, was in full occupation. So after 22 January, the only flight passage left open was the frozen Frische Haff. At its narrowest part it was 8 or 9km wide. But as it had to be crossed lengthways, the distance over the ice was 20 to 30km. Refugees later declared that the Frische Haff was by far the worst stretch of the journey, and from every account of refugees from East Prussia, West Prussia, Pomerania and Brandenburg one hears of the cold, the dangers and the muddle caused by the Nazi Gauleiters in forbidding any organised evacuation. Even when the Soviet army was only a few kilometres away, these men swore that there was no necessity for the people to leave home; and when the latter had the courage to start on their trek and had gone many difficult miles, some ran into

Soviet forces and were sent back to their devastated villages or, far worse, to Siberia in open cattle trucks.

Confusion grew upon confusion as the Russian army got nearer and the defending German army fought step by step backwards until homes and villages were a mass of ruins and rubble. By then people from the furthest parts of eastern Germany had been forced to save themselves and the trickle of refugees grew into a flood as they moved slowly westwards; slowly, because the speed of most of the refugee treks had to be regulated to the gait of the oxen, which also helped to pull the loaded waggons. In Pomerania and Mark Brandenburg the owners of the farms and estates were necessarily the last to leave; for several months they had remained behind to look after those worn, weary and sick newcomers.

It is no easy thing to decide when the moment has come to pack one's small handgrip, and leave everything one holds dear, the lovely old furniture which has taken on the gleam of a mirror through generations of polishing, the silver handed down from father to son, the family heirlooms, one's own personal possessions—perhaps very dear because the donor has died on a distant, frozen battlefield, uncared for and buried in an unknown grave. It is heart-breaking to leave the animals, the dogs—the Scottie who follows one from room to room, looking at one with his deep brown eyes hoping and pleading, and yet fearing he must be left behind! Some people did manage to take their dogs with them, some had them destroyed beforehand, but for others the moment of departure came too suddenly, often in the middle of the night. And some people thought the Allies would win the war quickly and in a few days, a week at most, they would be able to return; so they too went quickly, leaving their houses and gardens with fear in their hearts at what lay behind them and hope in their minds, towards the Allied Forces in the West. And all the time the Nazi radio blared that the war was nearly won and the enemy ringed in, even as a shell landed in the garden throwing up a cloud of dust and stones.

Refugees who came even later into these desolate villages said that it was one of the saddest sights and sounds to see and hear the unmilked cows, which had been turned out in their hundreds, free to roam at will but never free from the milk in their swollen udders. There were hungry and starving pigs, and house cats gone wild. Often they found shelled and burning houses with unburied dead or, upon opening a farm house door, the table laid for supper, or the unwashed remains of the last meal in the kitchen, relics of the moment when the occupants had left everything and hurriedly gone with their horses, their oxen and their waggons loaded with refugees. The waggons were often driven by strange women for there were practically no men on the great trek, which consisted chiefly of women, children and old people from East and West Prussia, Baltic families from Esthonia, Latvia and so on, and some Polish refugees and French, Dutch and British prisoners-of-war.

And in all this terrible helplessness, this fear, and this urgency to get away to the West to the hoped for shelter offered by the Allies, one is always told of the endurance of the horses, their courage and their willingness in the face of starvation and frightful cold. One hears of their brave efforts to get their human burden to safety through ice, snow, storm and axle-deep mud, plodding tiredly on for hundreds of miles, day after day, at night standing out still harnessed to their waggons, without shoes, bearing foals and losing them—but never willingly giving up. Some died by the way, making a last gallant effort to walk one yard

Page 71 A pair of Thoroughbred mares in harness at Maldeuten Stud; still the best method of transport in East Prussia

Page 72 (above) Two East Prussian mares which were rescued from the Don steppes where they had been taken as booty by Soviet troops at the end of the war; (below) the ruins of a church and rectory. Two armies passed by and the havoc left in their wake can be seen thirty years later

further on the congested road, some were captured, but some got through, thin, tired, dirty and perhaps lousy, foot-sore and collarsore. Yet they came all that distance at the walk, at the trot, skeletons of what they once were—skeletons of a breed of horses in whose veins runs the blood of Eclipse, skeletons with the blood and spirit to found a new tradition of fortitude, which put their old traditions of endurance and stamina for hunting, steeplechasing and farm work completely in the shade.

The following letters about the trek were lent to me by the Society of Breeders & Friends of the Trakehner Horse. They are from people whom I have never met, letters written without passion, all emotion drained out of them and it is almost beyond imagination to visualise the terribleness of the situation. These people slept out on the thawing ice of the Frische Haff, sometimes knee-deep in water, and where the ice suddenly gave way, horses, waggons and people went under. Low-flying planes added to the dreadful situation, for the bomb-holes were a trap to those trying to cross under cover of darkness. For many weeks many of the horses never came out of harness, many were in-foal mares, and almost all lived on only 3lb of corn per day; many were unshod because most of the blacksmiths had been called up and there was no iron for shoes. One and a half million horses died in Germany during the last war, and the fate of many East Prussian people is still unknown, but many, many thousands died trying to cross the Haff. Those who survived reached the British Forces weeks later, having journeyed about 900 miles.

Herr Franz Scharfetter writes:

'With regard to the performance of my mares on the trek, I should like to say that only my beautiful East Prussian

73

E

mares saved me from capture by the Russians.

'On 18 January 1945 I telephoned the County Farmers' Association, Insterburg, and asked if we must evacuate, and was told I could sleep quite happily, as in two days the Russians would be beaten back out of East Prussia. The next day early in the morning I was awakened by the army and was told that the enemy had broken through and were marching on Grünheide and Aulenbach. I immediately awoke the PoW as my own people had all gone to the Volksturm, so we fed and packed up everything and at 17 hours left my lovely Hengstenberg. The Russians were already in Aulenbach, 3km from my farm.

'I trekked with 21 mares, most of them carrying foals. For the first twenty-four hours I drove day and night without stopping to feed or water. I drove 40cwt loaded waggons with two in-foal mares harnessed to each. After one stop I went by Bartenstein (Alt Passarge) over the Haff, and made one march from Braunsberg to Danzig, I think this was 120km [75 miles!]. This was the longest day's journey. Because they were lame I had unfortunately to leave two mares in Mecklenburg. Often the mares had to remain outside day and night in the appalling snowstorms, but on the trek only one mare foaled. We daily marched 50 to 60km and many of my mares went as far as Mecklenburg without shoes.

'The food ration was daily 6lb oats per mare and some hay. My mares first miscarried after our arrival, when they had eight days rest. The reason for the still-born foaling is that at first they had no food, only some rye straw.'

Herr Albert Shenk tells us:

'I left Kreis Bartenstein on 28 January in driving snow

74

and above 20 degrees of frost with a waggon weighing over 40cwt. It was impossible even to think of finding shelter at night. For more than six weeks by day and night the horses were harnessed to the waggon without being taken out, and endured every kind of wind and weather. In January and February, when it would be impossible for two horses to go forward in the deep snow, four would be harnessed together. As we came near the Haff, it began to thaw, the ice was cracked and water stood over it. From the beach, the waggons went over with fifty yards distance between each waggon, one behind the other; many were not careful enough and drove too near each other and therefore many waggons were lost. Near Leisunen we drove on to the Haff, and thought only to drive across to the Nehrung, but we were not allowed on, and had to drive to Kahlberg, the whole distance of the Haff.

'We had to spend the night on the ice, and then came to a place where for about 200 yards the horses had to be driven through at the gallop—the ice rolled behind the waggon like waves of water. There were various unhorsed waggons which had been trailers and could not be taken through and had had to be left. Therefore I turned and drove back 7km to fetch them on to the Nehrung. For two days we drove through sand and hills and when two horses could not pull the load, others came to help.

'Then we had still two more days on the Baltic strand in the sand dunes, a difficult journey. When we reached Danzig at last, the horses had survived the worst; the roads were good although there were steep hills. We were sent to quarters in Pomerania and the horses had 4-5lb of oats per head per day. Until then one got nothing, one had to go 'begging'. My two mares were in foal, and two days after each other in Pomerania, when we had the worse part of

75

the journey behind us, their foals were born. The foals were completely developed but had starved to death before birth. There were days when we had done over 50km. Usually we made 30km per day and we arrived after a journey of nine weeks.'

Herr Heinrich Rosigkeit, a farmer from Angerburg, arrived with his five in-foal warm-blood mares and one half-bred mare. Herr Rosigkeit lived only for his horses; he was a master in the care of horses and so arranged it that his horses were kept in the best condition during the whole march. It is astonishing that they covered the distance without shoes. After the capitulation, with his mares Wally and Flagge he successfully took part, with borrowed waggon, in horse shows in Schleswig–Holstein.

Herr Rosigkeit says:

'I left at 16 hours on 29 January 1945 from Kreis Bartenstein, with three waggons each pulled by two horses. The main roads were so crowded with army lorries and troops, that I took to field cart-paths. The journey went Krekollen–Ratzen–Rendenau–Landsberg, from there by the cart path in the direction of Kl Steegen to the Haff and then along the Nehrung.

'The roads were blocked with driven snow, so that for the most part one had to drive over the sown fields. My waggons weighed 25cwt. I had loaded with much oats so that the mares could be well fed during the early part of the journey, as there was nothing to be had on the trek roads. At last, when we reached Pomerania we got 4-6lb oats, but sometimes only 2lb was to be bought. Of my seven mares, which I had with me, four were in foal. One mare foaled down three days before we left home, and the foal had to remain behind, the mare was harnessed to a waggon and came through the journey well. Two mares lost their foals on the journey. One mare who made the journey foaled down successfully here on 28 April.

'Until I had got over the Vistula, I drove day and night some 60km, otherwise usually 40-50km. It was very difficult to find stabling and generally the horses had to remain outside. Thanks to my care of the horses they withstood the journey well, with the exception of one who had laminitis and had to be shot.'

Herr Hans Schlemminger gives the following information:

'Journey from Schlossberg to Tapian, October 1944. From Tapian to Eutru, Holstein, January 1945. Roads generally very bad and hilly. Detours on cart tracks over the Haff from 28 January to 3 February, 1945.

'We left in driving snow and 23 degrees of frost, then cold rainstorms without ceasing. Food ration 3lb oats per day, usually no hay or straw. A third of the whole journey without night shelter, and without a day's rest, except for a halt of three weeks in Mecklenburg, where the horses had to work in the fields at once. Usually on the journey we stopped only when it became too dark and with dawn we went on. Removal of the harness or grooming was impossible.

'We crossed the Oder in a freezing rain storm and stood $2\frac{1}{2}$ days on the embankment. Four horses got colic from this exposure and had to be left behind. Longest day's journey 50km, average 20-25km, long harvest waggons weighing 50cwt pulled by pair horses. These well-bred in-foal mares came through, although all three lost their foals

77

after arrival here. Of fifteen horses at the commencement of our trek, four half-bred 4 year-old horses had to be left on the way because of weak hearts, because the waggons were overloaded following requisition (without compensation) of four waggons and ten horses by the Army and Home Guard near Königsberg. Of nine in-foal mares, all foals born dead. The waggons were driven by foreign men and women, as our own people had been called up.

'After the capitulation I had to sell six horses at dead loss, as there was no way of keeping them. And as soon as we arrived the horses had to go to work in the fields.'

Frau Marthe Hubner writes of how her two mares Selma and Mike, who was not yet quite 4, did an average 86km daily:

'We went over the Haff on 2 February 1945 and on the 22nd (just three weeks later) we were in East Hanover, near Rothenburg. In Kriwan, near Stolp in Pomerania we had one day's rest and also in Pinnow, near Prenzlau. We never did less than 60km per day. Food 10-15lb per mare, but from Kriwan only 5lb per day. Hay, when one could get it. Condition of the horses throughout good, although they were thin. After a few days in East Hanover they were asked to help in the fields!'

Annemarie Kneip says that her horses spent eighteen nights harnessed but free, and one night out on the Haff in 2ft of water.

Herr Arno Tummescheit says:

'It was amazing to see the endurance of the mare Spinne,

78

heavily in foal. She was near-wheeler in the first waggon, and showed not the slightest sign of tiredness. She allowed no other waggon to overtake her, and trotted on immediately on her own. She took part in everything and it was clear to see that tiredness was unknown to her.'

A letter to the Trakehner Society from Otto Baron von der Goltz, says:

'My wife and sister-in-law left in two carriages on 22 January 1945; icy conditions of roads, 16 degrees of frost. They covered around 1,000km and usually spent the night in draughty sheds. Food was sufficient as they came upon evacuated villages and could take what they wanted. The longest day's journey was 120km in 27hr; average about 50km daily. They had a landau with luggage and four people, pulled by Hansi and a gelding by Lindequist, and a rubber-wheeled waggon with luggage and two people. All the well-bred horses got through the trek, but two got swollen glands, the gelding badly.

'It is interesting perhaps that three of the horses had always been used as carriage horses, therefore were used to trotting; whilst Capriole had been used only for field work. There was no difference to their endurance although they trotted continuously, to which Capriole was not so used as the carriage horses. Hansi foaled three weeks before the trek began.'

Another farmer who made the trek observes that he left with 45 horses which included 10 yearlings and that the roads were deep with snow and icy conditions. Food was quite insufficient and sometimes the minimum ration of 3lb oats failed altogether, because there was none to be

79

had. The main roads often could not be used because of army movements. The bad cart-paths were most tiring for over-tired horses. He says:

'It is a wonder how the courageous animals brought us here, they gave their all. The endurance of our East Prussian horses was the more apparent, when one remembered that, for three months in our evacuation quarters, they always had insufficient food, 3lb daily, and so were in no proper condition to undertake the long march. One mare foaled in Kolberg on the evening of the march and the foal was born healthy. The mare had fever but next morning undertook the journey and came through well.

'The endurance of our East Prussian horses during the flight from our native land to the West is unparalleled. One can only hope and wish that in the re-building of our country an appropriate place will be found for them.'

Another refugee observes significantly that 'people living here can scarcely understand that the horses pulled waggons all the way here [Western Germany] from East Prussia'.

One of the final reasons for the failure of the Russian campaign—bearing in mind the extraordinary feat of the German armies in ever reaching the heart of Russia—and the dissolution and collapse of East Prussia lay, I am told, in the fact that neither defeat, failure, or retreat were contemplated for this meant defeatism. One can scarcely understand this attitude and can only accept it as a fact. As we have seen, no preparations had been made for a retreat. Such an event was never contemplated by the government, it was deemed a complete impossibility. Therefore, when it did occur, lacking any plan or thought, the whole procedure of the evacuation of the Province was a thorough shambles of retreating infantry; advancing tanks; refugees, horses, cattle on foot and in waggons blocking the roads, so that neither the one nor the other could come forward or go back—a sitting target for aircraft and pin-point gunfire. In England, on the other hand, one remembers all the anti-invasion plans, the organisation for evacuation, the marvel of the retreat from Dunkirk because all this had previously been envisaged as a possibility, even though no one imagined the probability of such a thing as occupation by a foreign power.

The chaos and the shambles of the war in East Prussia fails the imagination entirely, for such a frightful thing has never happened in the annals of history. An account or description of it is like a warm-water douche compared to the hell which millions of people and animals actually endured, or in which they finally lost their lives.

When I was collecting information for this book, I was having lunch with a friend in a small hotel in north Germany. The occasion was a meeting of members of the Trakehner Society who had gathered to look at the horses —a meeting of old friends and horse lovers, of people who had made that long trek under all sorts of conditions. Some chance remark of mine led to a lady sitting at a table nearby to turn to us and ask: 'You are interested in our horses?' I told her that it was the reason for my being there, and that I wanted some first-hand knowledge of the flight from East Prussia. 'I can give it to you,' she said, 'for I brought my four children and our horses safely out.'

Months went by, and I felt she must have forgotten her promise in the rush of work which is the lot of every refugee smallholder. But no! One morning a long letter arrived, it must have taken many precious hours to write, and it was written simply because I, a stranger and a foreigner, had asked for it. If only there were more of such a spirit of friendliness about in the world.

'You must surely think that I am not going to write to you but as the wife of a settler one always has so much to do and today is the first time I have sufficient peace to write.

'I will describe where we lived and worked in East Prussia. My husband owned a 500 acre farm in Darkehmen, which had been in the family's possession for 200 years. There we reared horses and cattle. We had nine good mares, supplied stallions to the Province, sold remounts and also young mares for breeding purposes, and riding horses.

'At the time when the Russian army was getting nearer, I lived with my five small children and my elderly invalid parents—my mother had been confined to her chair for ten years with rheumatism, and my father had a very sick heart and had to have injections every two days. We lived alone, with the wives of our workers and a few Belgian prisoners-of-war.

'The thunder of gunfire came nearer and nearer, until one day in October we heard the sound of battle all around us. It was an extraordinarily queer feeling. I begged my parents to go to safety, and I would have liked to have given them the children too, but it was forbidden. The children had to remain where I was, and I had to stay at my post. But at last my parents decided to go, and they went with their two horses and their housemaid and took with them my 6 year-old daughter Susanne.

'On the 20 October 1944 all the inhabitants of neighbouring Goldap went past on the road. We were fearfully excited because we knew then that only 2km (1¼ miles) away the Goldap district was emptied of people. I spent a sleepless night. The next morning the leader of the farmers in our district rang me up and ordered me to evacuate. At 11.30 I had to be at a neighbouring farm with all my people, and together we were to begin our trek.

'A wild packing began. I allocated, to the wives and their families, one waggon for two families. The maids and I loaded one waggon with our things. One of the Belgians had to slaughter a pig, which we loaded just as it was, to be dealt with later. We let loose the cows with their calves, which were in the cowhouses, and drove them to the herd. Unfortunately the calves were not used to sucking, and it was a terrible thing to leave all these animals to their fate.

'The unforgettable thing was the quiet calm of my son Wolfgang. To his great joy he found the bookcase door open, and sat down quietly in a chair and read. Barbara, our little horse-lover was only 4, and early that morning was sitting quietly on the milk-horse as the cow-shed was being cleaned—I can still see her. She asked an odd question, whilst we were packing, when she saw that the little cot with her 5 month-old sister was put to one side: "Aren't we going to take Dolly with us?"

'We were about to get ourselves into the waggon when my 10-year-old son Eberhard appeared on his bicycle from Darkehmen where he went to school and was a boarder. He cried bitterly for he was the only one of the children who fully understood what was happening.

'Just as we were waiting for everyone else in the neighbouring village, someone arrived and said we should return home, as we could not start before next day. Bitter as my parting from home was, and happy as I had been there, I decided never to return. I should never have been able to sleep for fear.

83

'Because the streets were blocked, we had only bad cart-roads in front of us. The first night of our flight we spent about 20km from Upballen and, as I had tied a cow to a waggon, we cooked a milk soup; first the children were fed and the adults ate the remainder. I should have been completely despondent if my children had not been with me and their presence, especially when I had the 5-month-old Dorothea in my arms, seemed to help to keep me quiet and to give me new courage.

'Quite near Gerdauen one of our prisoners, Anton, came to me—he was always helpful and kind—and said: "Madame, quick go on, otherwise the tanks come."

'It was quite impossible to go on quickly, because all the roads had been closed for the army; we had to use completely over-filled roads and byways. We did not stop all that night, we went on as quickly as possible and found out a few days later that the Russians had only been held up by a few of the Home Guard, otherwise they would have broken through and cut us off. What a dreadful fate was spared us!

'One day as we were about to deal with the pig, a nearby town was bombed, in great fear we jumped into our waggons and hurried on.

'On 24 October we spent the night with a friend who was a great rider, and our horses were well looked after. Next day I joined my parents who were staying with relations, all of whom were astonished at the appearance of my children and my mares.

'Now of course, I began to realise the full pain of losing my country and my home, and the women kept on remarking that we were homeless. Suddenly I became so ill that I had to look for a doctor. But we went on, and reached an old friend of my father with whom we stayed two days and

I was unable to leave my bed. People and animals were looked after well. As we neared Pr Holland, the local Gauleiter ordered all refugees to stop and seek quarters with local farmers and, as my dear parents had got to the end of their strength, I stayed there and begged a lady, who was a renowned horse lover, to find us a place. We stayed from 30 October until 21 January and the horses and my parents and children were really looked after. My people and two waggons and teams of four helped with the sugar-beet harvest.

'On our first Sunday there we had a visit from a doctor and his daughter who had fled from Hamburg, to escape the bombing, and who was now with her parents in the Mohrungen district. I had sent the doctor some yearlings, and some cases of things. They brought a wonderful cake and wanted to console us, but they did not know what fate had in store for them. The doctor told us that he and his wife would remain on their estate even if the Russians came. But his daughter and her little children were to return to Hamburg. We never met again. After the collapse [of Germany] I heard that they had delayed their departure because the old people wanted to accompany them in the waggon. It was too late, the Russians overtook them, and they were so terrified that they all took their own lives. Even today I am deeply shocked that these dear, tactful and cultivated people had such an end.

'During this time I returned twice to Upballen, and was horrified to see how our soldiers had ransacked the place— foreign troops could scarcely have done worse. Furniture had been thrown into the cellar and mattresses had been hauled into the house, and they were using our dining room as a cinema. In the paddock I found a strange horse grazing and the lonely animal badly wanted company.

Our valuable herd of cows and the bull which we had bought for £750 were all missing. I had, of course, taken the horses with me. The courtyard was full of pigeons and none of the Home Guard was there to thrash the corn. A puppy belonging to our St Bernard bitch and the dachshund which I had given to a neighbour had come back, and this faithful little thing could scarcely contain himself for joy when he saw me again. My heart was dreadfully heavy as I went away. Were we to lose everything and never return?

'Two well-mannered young officers accompanied me some of the way, and I told them of my dejection. One of them said that one must never hang on to one's possessions. He had always carried with him private possessions from which he could not bear to be parted, until one day in an acute emergency he had thrown them all into the Don. And I had exactly the same feeling in Mecklenburg after five weeks flight. But I was exceptionally lucky that my five children were alive and that my husband was a PoW in England.

'At the beginning of January Dr Schilke rang me up and asked if I didn't want to send my mares on to Mecklenburg, which I certainly did, but the Russians were all about us again. The front on the Vistula had been broken through and they were pouring in through East Prussia. At this time my father was dreadfully ill and through nightwatch and fear, I was completely done up and stupid. The weather was suddenly wintry, with clouds of snow, frost and icy roads. Once more, on 20 January 1945 we had orders to pack up and evacuate and we had to shoe the horses hurriedly. I had no iron and my old man Christokat (who was 70) and the two Belgians shod the horses with shoes from the iron which the village provided. Most of my mares were in foal and had not been driven for several months.

'A period of suffering without equal began for us all—humans and animals. Undoubtedly my fur gloves, a present from my husband saved me. The Russians were always on our heels. Late in the afternoon we passed through Elbing and in the night thirty Russian tanks arrived in the town. We were in quarters in Neuteich and during the night got the alarm; we hurriedly dressed and went on further, ever further. The roads were ice smooth, and we saw many waggons which had slipped into the ditches. The previous evening my mother had almost turned over with my baby. My dying father had stopped the closed carriage driven by the maid, at a house, and a man passed with a bundle of hay. The horses were starving and followed him, and in a moment the carriage had slipped into a ditch. I was driving the last trek waggon, with the four other children, and was horrified when I came up. By chance a cattle dealer from Darkehmen was also there and he sympathised with me and suggested we should pull it out with chains and other horses—unhappily we pulled the carriage apart.

'Now we had to get my crippled mother out and carry her into the house, and I went to the farmers in the village to beg them to help us to fit my country carriage with a cover so that my parents and children could have some protection from the cold and snow. I had to return exhausted to the house and my family without accomplishing this. But shortly afterwards a farmer arrived to say he would do it early next morning. I was standing as if frozen to the wall as he spoke to me, and came to with a start at the sound of his voice—I had gone to sleep standing up.

'During these days I was quite certain that we could not survive. But at last we got near an emergency bridge

87

over the Vistula at Kunsendorf; it had been erected only two days. On the embankment waggons were driven three abreast, but luckily soldiers were guarding it to keep order. I had the entire family in the carriage, the baby lay behind on a cushion on my mother's lap while in front, on the coachman's seat, my two boys sat and sometimes took over the driving. We were driving on the outside line when we saw a Blackcap [a German national from Russia] who was trying to overtake us and would have rammed our waggon and turned us over into the river. My cry of horror brought a soldier who made the man stop.

'The whole day our trek-party had got more and more apart and we had to wait ages, on the other side of the bridge, for the work people to catch us up. But my father was so ill that I left Eberhard on the bridge to await them, and went to the nearest farm for help. As soon as my parents and children were being cared for, and the horses fed, I went back to Eberhard. It was already dark and I looked everywhere for him and couldn't find him; dreadfully depressed I went back to my mother who sat sleepless in the waggon in the barn—I could not lift her out of the waggon alone.

'Then the awful bombing of Marienburg by the Soviet troops began, and so after a while I returned to the bridge and Eberhard came to meet me. He had seen nothing of the other waggons, I took him into my arms, and there in the early dawn, fear of our own fate overwhelmed us again.

'There was a dreadful snowstorm during the next few days and we went to Bütow and Berend, where the horses had to sleep out under the sky as I could not find them a stable. I covered them with our fur rugs but next morning found them covered in icicles and frozen snow on their

Page 89 (above) The beautiful church of Heiligelinde, the Holy Linden; (below) East Prussia is a 'land of a thousand lakes'; a view of the Löwentinsee in the heart of Masuria, at Lötzen

Page 90 (above) A lake, a hamlet and a great forest which was once inhabited by elk; (below) an unending vista across one of Europe's most beautiful provinces

flanks. Alwine, a lovely golden chestnut, was due to foal in March and I very much afraid she would cast the foal. I laid my hand on her sides and to my joy felt the foal's movement, and it gave me courage.

'We stayed in a school, and my parents were put in the first-aid room where there were many people suffering from frost-bite; after much persuasion we were allowed to stay with them and we all slept wonderfully in one bed. Then I nearly lost Barbara. I wanted to wash and the child ran along behind me; when I had finished I forgot all about her—and then of course she was lost. We searched everywhere, through all the rooms, until at last a man said: "If you are looking for a child, there's one asleep here." And there she was!

'The loss of the other trek waggons made itself felt, I had no nappies for the baby and no more food and sugar, and the child lived for fourteen days on rye bread soaked in milk. We had no change of clothes and felt horrible. Once we came through a village where the day previously twenty-five children had been buried in the snow in the ditch bordering the road.

'Next day as we were driving along, the little one began to scream and my mother thought perhaps she was freezing to death. I went hot and cold and sprang out of my seat to see, but she had been too tightly packed in and might have been suffocated if I had not looked. It was really dreadful trying to drive through deep snow, sometimes the poles broke and often the roads were blocked and had to be cleared.

'In Bütow we stayed at the hospital, which was a good thing for the children, and the mares were fed with bread by the kindly sisters. There I met two old friends, one of whom was terribly sad as her grandchild had just died.

91

'We then had to turn northwards to Stolp because cannon fire could be heard to the south. The snow and frost were not so bad, but the stony roads were awful for the unshod horses, whose hooves began to bleed. I managed to get them shod. But Lorchen, the children's pony, ran along happily, unshod. We were taken in by the village blacksmith, himself the father of nine children and they had very little room, but they gave us their best room, and his wife fried us potatoes, and there was milk soup with custard powder—it was a wonderful meal. Next day the smith shod Lorchen and his wife gave us a large sausage. I wonder what happened to these people later.

'One day it poured and poured with rain and at night I got my father into an armchair in a house, my mother slept in the carriage as was usually the case and the children and myself in the hall. Next day it was freezing hard and the boys and I suffered agonies as our wet feet froze.

'One evening we landed up in a village where the good people cooked us potatoes and rissoles, and horses and children were cared for, and although we were used to lying on the bare floor in our fur coats, we found we could change and for once sleep in beds. These people had understood what it was like for us, since the carriage was our only home.

'We and our faithful horses and our St Bernard dog Donna had become a complete family. Every morning when we harnessed up the horses we had to bring them all out of the stable together, none of them wanted to remain alone in a strange stable. In the afernoons, everytime we passed a farm, they looked at it and then round at us as if to inquire: "Are we stopping the night here?" Mealtimes were in the morning and at night for us and the animals; it was dreadfully tiring for my parents, but we all felt better when we were in the carriage driving further on.

'Near the Oder we had bad luck and two wheels broke, it meant a loss of two days. We felt it would be safer with the Oder behind us and so we always tried to press on but we came to a bad bit of road, such enormous holes that I thought the axle would break. I was glad my parents could not see through the cover over the carriage. The boys went in front and cut grass and held it in front of the horses' noses to encourage them to pull. Many horses could go no farther and their owners were stuck. I wanted to hug our beloved horses and we breathed more freely when they got us through, for Senta and Alwine had not left us in the lurch.

'After this we had the crossing of the Oder. In the evening light it was almost sinister as we, the first carriage to go, drove on to the ferry. The ferrymen saw my fear and once it had started, they came over and held the horses, thank God! Then, in the dark, we began the uncanny drive through ruined villages, falling into bomb-holes, and once we drove on the railway line, but managed to find the road again and in spite of extreme fatigue at long last we reached Falkenberg. Here we found an empty room, which was bad for my father because he could not lie on the floor. Senta had become much thinner, but Alwine always looked well and was much admired, it was clear she would soon foal down.

'As my father needed injections every two days, I called at a hospital and asked to be taken in, but although the porter was sympathetic she refused. So I had to ask for the matron and, when she heard of our condition, she allowed us in and saw that we could have baths. We each had a bed to ourselves, and regular mealtimes. The horses got bread and Donna a real meal, it was wonderful being with people again; two days later we gratefully said goodbye. I heard later that the poor nurses were shockingly used by the Russians.

'On the journey through Mecklenburg we usually met helpful kindly people, and on 27 February we finally arrived at my sister's place of refuge. My parents were completely finished and my father had to be taken to hospital in Dobbertin where he died six days later. His beloved Trakehner horses took him to his last resting place.

'I found quarters in Mestlin with some wonderful people who helped in every way they could. Little Susanne had developed a bad heart through all the fear and discomfort, but here she was able to recover a little. The baby had cut her teeth and improved with fresh air and nursing. But the horses were so well looked after and it seemed that Alwine would have her foal in peace. But the Russians still came nearer and we had to go on. Luckily I managed to collect Annelise and take her with me. The workpeople had left her in the district because she was foaling; I found out in time, but the foal died. Alwine's foal had to be left behind, and we had to milk her, but in spite of caring for her she became very obstinate and sometimes wouldn't pull. But one night we could get no milk, so we used mare's milk for the baby's porridge and it tasted very nice.

'Once near Schwerin we came to a bombed bridge and we had to wait a long time; when at last we could go on Alwine refused to move. A man came along and started to hit her and if the mare had jumped forward we should all have been overturned down a slope. I begged him instead to help push, other people helped too, and the mare quietened down and began to pull.

'The road really was dreadful, and the horses' harness badly broken and mended with string—any unusual movement would have torn it completely apart. Sometimes we were caught by low-flying aircraft and the boys and I were always listening for the whistle of falling bombs. Once my son and I were looking for shelter in a field, and the dog Donna was with us; but when she realised that the carriage and horses remained behind she ran back and stayed to guard them. One day I stopped at a farm to rest and went to talk to the owners, when there suddenly appeared an aeroplane which shot at our carriage with the five children inside. I was quite terrified but, thank God, he missed them all although the bullet holes were to be seen in the walls of the barn. The horses stood there so tired and still that I had difficulty in getting them under the nearest trees.

'Next day British soldiers entered the village and I was detained there for four weeks, then I was allowed to go on to join our people near Neustadt, where the other horses were and all our luggage; but not much was to be found for the work people had used everything they had wanted —even my shoes. I had only my riding boots and from then on we all had to wear wooden clogs!

'I lent the other eight horses to strangers, who used them to replace their cars, one of them Beatekind was useless for further breeding and I had to sell her just before the currency reform, for bread. Alwine, the wonderful chestnut mare, who had endured the trek on the shortest rations and had always looked well under awful conditions, died of starvation on a farm in Holstein—it happened six months before we got our little holding. I went to see her during her last days, and she greeted me with a soft friendly nicker. If only I had had the means, I believed I could have saved her. Senta, another lovely mare, received a fork in her shoulder and died from the injury. Prima foaled on the trek and did not cleanse, the work people failed to call in a veterinary surgeon, and used her every day and so she died eight days later. As it is, out of the eight horses which I thought I had saved only the descendants of the Andacht family have survived. It is very difficult to rear horses on a settler holding—there's not enough room, and the whole time one must try to get money to pay the rent.

'This is an account of our flight, perhaps you will never use it, but if you do write of our experiences in your book, I would so much like to have it.'

CHAPTER SIX

Survival in Western Germany

DURING ALL those weeks on the trek, the one fixed thought in everybody's minds was that if they could reach the West they would be safe. Probably very few of them gave much time to wondering what would become of them, once they had arrived. The shock of so suddenly leaving home, the fright and the hunger and tiredness, left nothing in their numbed minds but the will to survive, and the effort which survival entailed left no place for speculation on the future.

Many people therefore met with bitter disappointments. They found that the people in the West were engrossed in their own problems, which occupation by Allied troops forced on them, and some had not much time or sympathy for these newcomers suddenly forced upon their already strained means. Let it be truthfully said, very few people welcome evacuees thrust upon their homes and lives, and very few evacuees make happy guests. Of course there are exceptions, but it is the most difficult thing in the world to allow oneself to be dependent upon strangers, and refugees at any time are in a most unfortunate position. And in this case, these unhappy people came into a part of their own country which was itself torn by war and faced with the problem of foreign armies. Where food was already

97

short, and accommodation at a minimum; the refugees had very little money to keep themselves, and they brought with them horses which also needed keeping to a land well supplied with its own breeds of horses! It was a very difficult situation.

It was a topsyturvy world too, this period before the currency reform. Part of Western Germany was occupied by British forces, another part by American, and a third by the French, all with their own rules and regulations for the inhabitants. You could not move from one Occupied Zone to another without passes which were hard to obtain at the best of times. And in Mecklenburg, when the people thought themselves safe under the British, they found that they and the territory had been handed overnight to the Russians, and it was with the utmost difficulty that some, for whom it was unsafe to remain, managed to go on and cross the Elbe and get into Western Germany. One of the most incredible sights to be observed early one morning in Thuringia was when the American army marched out and the Soviet army marched in.

And an equally odd though perhaps pleasanter situation was to be found in Schleswig–Holstein, where a completely mobilised regiment of German soldiers, under their own officers, in full uniform with arms and vehicles, was maintained for at least six months after the end of the war, to help the British troops keep order and police Northern Germany. A British major lived in one house with his German counterpart living next door—and each had his own sentry posted outside.

Gradually the newcomers were absorbed into the countryside and into the community generally, but alas, the horses paid the toll of superfluity. Their owners were forced to lend them to work on the fields to get in the harvest. They had no respite and still not much to eat. Perhaps there was not much to give them, but one is beset by the thought that much, much more could have been done for those horses. After all, there were so few survivors.

Out of 56,000 horses in East Prussia only 1,000 got to the West and fewer still survived the aftermath of war. Some of the opprobrium must fall upon the Forces of Occupation, for they came, after all, from horse loving nations. But it is fair to say that there were one or two men in positions in the British army who did as much as they were able to help these horses and their owners; and their names are remembered with affection today by those people to whom their help meant so much.

So, still toiling on, unrecognised in the main for their gallant rescue, except for the further work of which they might be capable, separated from their owners whose hearts were broken because they had no option but to accept the situation, more of these beautiful animals collapsed and died. It seems a dreadful thing to have allowed to happen. Thank God! not many of us in England have seen either people or horses starve to death. It is a sight which haunts the memory for evermore.

One man who got to the West had a very difficult time. He had got his horses safely through, but after the capitulation had to sell six of them at cut prices, as there was no way of keeping them. As soon as he arrived the horses had to go to work in the fields.

Another refugee observes in a letter to the Trakehner Society: 'The mares were in foal, but they arrived in good condition. After two days they had to go to work and today [1945] are by no means in the good condition in which they arrived. A few days after their arrival the horses were examined by the army and, because they looked so well, the authorities wanted to take all three. After lengthy begging they only took one mare for whom I never received any payment.'

Some of the people who came to the West found work which could keep them and their horses. One of them, a young woman wrote to me and her account of her life in the West in the days of post-war occupation forms the basis of this chapter.

'Guided by the trek leaders, most of the treks came to the West without a particular end in view until at the end they were sent in one direction or another. Our trek did have an objective and this was the estate of friends of my former boss [the writer had been an agricultural student in 'Swiss' Holstein]. When we arrived the cowslips were in full bloom and all around us was the most beautiful countryside. But I had no eyes for it, I felt quite awful. This day meant at one and the same time the end of one period in one's life and the beginning of another. And for me it meant the end of something which was a part of my life. The long drive had given us the consciousness of the remnants of our personal freedom and accorded us country folk our deep wish "to be independent"—even if it were only a carriage with a horse in front.

'The future looked grey. The search for work in a country overfilled with people and horses, homesickness and worry, all the things that we had pushed aside would now become reality. We unharnessed the horses and my companion went off to her relatives. And I stood in the stable and cried like a little girl who is away from home for the first time.

'The grey mare munched her oats and now and again rubbed me with her white mealy nose. But it was so comforting just to have her still. I did not yet know that this day was the commencement of a spring and summer that was to be not only bitter and humiliating but at the same time would be described as a rich and almost happy one.

'First of all I had to prove the right of existence of my grey mare and myself. We carried anything anywhere—wood for new furniture for refugee families, vegetables and potatoes. We clambered up and down the steep hills on the estate where we were quartered. There was a big gathering in the market place of a nearby town where refugee horses were valued and hired out. The little brown mare, who had come part of the trek with my grey mare and myself, went to the army, but after the capitulation her owner finally lost sight of her. I stood by with my heart beating as the horses were run past—but I took my grey mare back home with me—perhaps people had more heart than I gave them credit for.

'We were allocated work on a farm and there I found a friend who had come from Pomerania with two horses, and during the next months we shared our joys and sorrows together with our horses.

'Both of us had been agricultural pupils and were used to farm and field work, but sometimes it was very hard. Usually we were hungry because the country people hadn't enough food to feed so many refugees, and they had lost their sense of what was possible for others. The work which I had to do, even though here on a smallholding I am now used to hard work, was beyond what I would expect any girl to do for me today. In the evening after ten hours work, we had to go over the books and work out the costs, or we had to search for hours for foals and young horses which had broken out of their meadows because of low-flying aircraft. Very early in the morning and very late at night we saw after our own horses, and the grey stood it best of all.

101

'Each horse was allowed 3lb of corn daily, and as much hay and straw as we liked to take. The first time that someone else tried to drive the grey she behaved so badly that afterwards only I took her out. She jibbed at the top of a hill and then as the driver tried to force her on, she stood and kicked until she was brought back to her stable. I was very glad about it!

'Sometimes we had long journeys. One journey to collect young trees for forestry work was 90km there and back, and we did it with only four hours rest. Later we received orders to drive by night (to try and avoid hedge-hopping aeroplanes) to take some refugees to other quarters. Since it seemed to me to be very dangerous I said the grey showed up too much in the dark, and so I got a brown horse which didn't belong to me, to drive.

'On our farm Poles, White Russians and Ukrainians, who had come with various treks, were working. The old foreman gave out the work in the morning, first in dialect for the natives and then in German for these strangers, but often they misunderstood him and were most unhappy when they had done something wrong. I understood only German, but I translated it for them every morning in my bad Polish, and so won their friendship. "You, Miss, only one horse," with my one grey mare they counted me amongst the peasants, "you're no capitalist, you come back with us when we go home." I thanked them. We had just come to the West for fear of little father Stalin! But they all went back to their native lands, probably to a very sad fate.

'One of them gave me a precious home-made cigarette, wrapped up in a letter written in Russian. I smoked it with decorum like a pipe of peace. I had grown up in the so-called corridor between Poland and Germany, but since the atrocities against us Germans in 1939, I had never got over the fear of their hate and cruelty. So here, in a strange country, we sealed our friendship.

'Our horses had stables at the back of the barn. There we spent the evenings of the last days of the war, looking out over the Baltic Sea at the burning ships full of refugees. We listened to the squadrons of bombers overhead and in the sinisterness of this débâcle as we stood beside our horses, the dream of the "thousand-year Reich" [promised by Hitler] came to an end.

'After the capitulation the British took over our country-side and closed an area about as big as a county, in which, as if in a big prison, German soldiers awaited their discharge. Every village and every farm was allocated a unit of troops, with their own officers, and with model discipline they organised themselves in barns, tents and huts. One saw soldiers everywhere. There were about 1,000, sometimes 2,000 on our farm. They were starving, for provisions were very short and what the civil population could give them never went round. They came from all over Germany, and like us refugees they had no news of their homes or relatives. The postal service came much later.

'We were once more able to breathe freely now that the shooting had come to an end, and the sadness for our ruined, divided country and worry about near and dear relatives and the future bound us all together. The difference between us, refugees and soldiers and the inhabitants, was the fact that the latter could take the ending of the war in the stride of their everyday lives after a comparatively undisturbed life during the war. And those who honestly tried to help in the changed position and put things right met with great difficulty. We had undergone such a great shock that the outward circumstances of everyday life was

103

of no particular concern. This present life was a transition which we had to take as it came. And this freedom from daily worry, this "gipsy" feeling, showed itself in the astonishing things which appeared in this concentrated mass of people.

'Everywhere the urge to create showed itself. Musicians held little gatherings, artists were to be seen sitting on the hillsides overlooking the sea, a young writer retired to the lighthouse and wrote. Variety artists and others with talent gave entertainments which would have done them credit in any city. They had a grateful public. The most successful, however, were the concerts. It wasn't so much that well-known people were on the platform; it lay in the audience who were starved of beauty after all the horror, and the freedom such beauty gave from their daily lives.

'I will never forget these evenings. Nor the conversations we had which lasted far into the night. Discussions about politics, social questions, about the characteristics and diversity of the German race, whose representatives were gathered together here, and the many and varied spiritual problems which would come with our occupation by neighbour nations. These conversations were based on the broad spectacle of the past and continued into the future and almost completely excluded the present. Now I often think how much has become reality of what was then only envisaged as spiritual development by these people.

'This experience, concentrated as it was into the short hours of a Sunday and the free evening hours to curfew, knitted us to the horses. At the beginning we were told we could not ride, so that other working people should not be annoyed at the sight of us. But one day when we saw our employer's daughter gallop out of a nearby wood, we regarded this prohibition lifted. We had no bicycles, and in the evenings on foot, we could only go short distances.

'So now we rode our horses! We had no saddles and we did not miss them. When we rode to a concert in the evening, or had accepted an invitation, we packed a skirt in a bag which we hung on our arms, took a halter and rope and tied our horses up somewhere where we could change quickly. And in those happy canters in order to arrive at our destination on time, and in the still rides home in the dark afterwards, we felt at one with the evening quietness and we experienced something from the old quotation "Paradise on earth lies on a horse's back".

'Sometime in July we got the postal service, through which by degrees we heard from friends and relatives. I belonged to those fortunates who found their parents and relatives were living in the West. But the other refugee girls on the estate—there were five of us—heard nothing certain and wanted to leave in order to try to join their relations. We had worked only for our food and lodging and now we had to think about earning money. We wanted to leave together and part once the Elbe was crossed.

'At first we had to seek a way out of our prohibited area. We walked long distances to see high English officials but we received no permits to leave. And it was also uncertain if the bridges over the Elbe were free for civilian traffic. On Sundays we rode the length of the frontier, hoping somewhere in the woods to find an unguarded corner where the vehicles could get through, but the frontier was too well guarded.

'Then the German army came to our help. A resourceful person had a permit written out for two refugee waggons, that they were in the service of the German army and must collect an X-ray apparatus from a town on the other side of the Elbe. A staff officer was to lead the expedition; before

105

the end of the war no officer would have been prepared to undertake such an adventure. Now we felt we were "conquered", but we did not mind getting round the numerous prohibitions and rules which had hung over us so long, provided no harm came to anyone.

'We had fourteen days to prepare, for which I got leave from work, and so I had time to get the waggons and harness ready. We had eaten only 1½lb of bread a week, the remaining rations we exchanged for leather and wood. A friendly saddler had made me a pair of traces and breechings for the grey mare, so that a single horse had an easier job to pull, as the waggons were made for a pair of horses. But I didn't quite trust the grey to pull alone as she had just become ill. So I made up my mind quickly and bought a second horse—a little chestnut East Prussian, who matched the grey well, and seemed tough and to have plenty of stamina. I stabled him with friends until we were ready to leave. I thought perhaps later I could hire out the pair more easily than I could the grey alone.

'This time our trek was to consist of two light pair-waggons, accompanied by three cyclists, and because we had not had a very easy time in our jobs we called it "the flight from Holstein!" We were in high spirits and looked forward to the journey. This trek had plenty of difficulties, but all the misfortunes were of a fairly cheerful nature and I will tell the story, although it has nothing to do with the flight from the Russians.

'The first misfortune happened two days before we were due to leave as I made a round of farewell visits on the chestnut. Two days before I had crossed a moor on foot and thought the way was quite safe—as I rode homewards on my chestnut he sank under me. He was belly-deep in the swamp and in fear tried to jump forwards, but only got

Page 107 A herd of three-year-old fillies at Liski (Liskien) Stud. This Stud is situated on the border which now divides East Prussia or Masuria, between Poland and the USSR

Page 108 (above) Brood mares working the medium light soil ready to drill; (below) Tarpan grazing off reeds in the Spirding Lake

himself deeper into it. I was on safe ground but could not stop the frightened animal until at last he reached a tree root. There he stood, but I didn't trust myself to let go of the reins, in order to try and find a safe path out of this morass. Night fell and nobody came near us. After curfew one could no longer hear even voices in the distance. So I decided to cry for help into the moonlit night. And I was lucky. A unit of soldiers came and brought bundles of wood and made a safe pathway out.

'But the chestnut suffered badly from this accident. Next day he was not well, and on the day we left we didn't like the look of him at all. By the time we arrived at our first stopping place for the night, he was seriously ill.

'At the first frontier control, we were sent back with our rather questionable papers—the next one allowed us through! In high spirits we had declared that we would live in the woods on berries if we couldn't get through, but we were glad when we knew we could go on. On the main road beyond the frontier we knew of an old low sheep-shed which looked as if it had sunk into the ground to a level with its roof. We had arranged this as a meeting place with our cyclists who had circled round the control post.

'When we arrived they had got permission of the farmer to allow us to stay the night in this shed. With the straw roof low over our heads, and the horses' heads showing in the soft light of our oil lamp we spent the first happy night of our freedom.

'But after this journey the chestnut was seriously ill and we had to take him the same evening to the nearest town to a veterinary surgeon, who gave him an injection and ordered complete rest. Complete rest for a horse on trek, who was supposed to cover 160km in three days right through Hamburg and over the Elbe!

109

'We had to have time. Nobody would take on an ill horse, and to help him we decided everyday only to drive as far as the next village; but in order not to create suspicion we let it be understood that we had come a great distance. It would have been best for the sick animal if we could have stayed longer in one place, but that wasn't possible. We had neither sufficient food for ourselves nor the horses, there were, as yet, no food coupons to be had, harvest had only just begun, and people had long since given away what had been left over from the previous year, so we could not expect anything from anyone.

'This first evening we still hoped that the chestnut would soon feel better. The grey mare who was also weak had valiantly come through. In order to earn our keep, we made lively plans, for in my rucksack I had the Punch and Judy puppets. With them we had already contributed to a children's play, which had been got up by the soldiers' organisation, so we knew how to work them together. We painted a notice board with a nice verse that Punch was on trek and wanted to play for the children; he was very hungry and although he was unwilling to charge he could only play if he were given something to eat! We were on a good thing. There was a horse stew from a fallen horse, that was being shared out and a peasant wife gave us a share for the journey. It was a great treat in these times and we had decided that come what might our good tempers would not be upset.

'In the morning we changed round. To my waggon we fitted the single shafts, which was then drawn by the strong brown horse of my friends. The grey mare paired with the other, although their only similarity was their colour. One cycle came on the waggon and our staff doctor with the heart injections in his first-aid kit and one of the other girls

110

led the chestnut slowly into the next village. On the following days he would only allow himself to be pushed forwards
with lengthy pauses, and before starting he always had to
have a heart injection. So we only covered 3-4km daily!

'We also actually found lodgings sometimes with nice
people who invited us to a meal and listened to the story
of the preceding winter and our flight from the Russians,
from which they had been mercifully spared. Or we made
our own arrangements in a hay barn. The first Punch show
was a great success for the children had not had much enter-
tainment during the last few years. We hung a tilt over our
stage made out of wood and poles and arranged wooden
seats, and these were overfilled. The first time we made an
error in organisation, for before the show we had forgotten
to make arrangements to receive their contributions—in
any case it was a painful proceeding—and their little offer-
ings of bread wrapped badly in this paper shortage, and
little bars of oats and sugar, were crumpled to nothing during the excitement of Punch's play. So the horses received
most of the contributions!

'Up to our arrival in Hamburg we played seven times.
We were so long on the road, and the shows were good for
our horses because the children's pleasure was shared by the
parents, and we received not only oats from the people with
whom we stayed but other farmers brought some over with
them. Everyday we lived better and better and in spite of
the short distance covered daily, our whole day was filled
up. We let the horses graze on the road verges, and ourselves searched for blackberries which were numerous.
Everything was washed and brushed, the horses and especially the grey mare had to be spotlessly clean—cooking during these starvation days assumed the greatest importance.

'Our staff doctor accompanied us as far as the Elbe bridge

with the papers for the crossing. His appearance at our first quarters seemed to trouble our hostess. With an earnest face she asked: "Now which is your wife?" He pointed to the most striking of us, and we kept him to it as it gave a trustworthy note to our trek. The doctor's "wife" at first blushed when she heard her unaccustomed name, but very soon without a flicker she told them all about the house in Berlin, the long and painful separation from her "husband" and the great pleasure they had when they finally met again —in such times one soon learnt to be disingenuous!

'Perhaps that is only the first step to dishonesty, but all the same my conscience is clear for all of us. Only once in Pomerania did I take hay secretly and that was because the people there would not even give us feeding-straw, although they threw it around freely for their cows. I will never forget the shock, when we had crept into the loft and found other people standing there. But how we laughed! The others were also pinching hay!

'Towards evening on the fifth day the chestnut looked better, he was anxious to eat his hay and his eyes were clear, but early next morning when I went into the stable he lay dead beside the grey mare. He looked quite contented, almost as if he were glad that all the bother of the journey lay behind him and it could not concern him any more. But I was very upset. We gave the burgomaster ten marks and asked him to have the chestnut buried.

'Now we travelled a bit faster, we spent the night on the outskirts of Hamburg, so that we could go through the town the next day, and never before had we been treated so well. It was quite different to what we had experienced in Holstein where they were either completely disinterested or showed only pity. The Hamburg people recognised us as fellow sufferers, and in the same way that they bore

112

the suffering of the great bombing [400,000 killed in four nights] without making a great to-do about it, so we tried not to give the impression of a sad and weary trek. Next day as we drove through the city people in the streets laughed and waved at us.

'We crossed the Elbe bridge without any trouble. Beyond in the wooded hills lay the Hamburg summer-house of a refugee family whom we had arranged to see and there we had our last misfortune. We stayed in a valley in a farmer's house, and in the evening rode over the hills to a small farewell party at our friends' house. We tied the horses with halters and chains to nearby trees. It was a tremendous treat to walk into a well-kept room with beautiful china—these things belonged to a life which we hadn't enjoyed for months. It was a farewell to a happy journey and everybody looked forward to the future.

'Then, as it began to grow dark outside, the children shouted that the horses were missing. There really were two loose chains hanging on the tree—only my grey mare was there! The horses stolen!

'In great anxiety we began to search. But nobody had seen them. Two of us borrowed bicycles and hurried to the burgomaster, the others searched the wooded paths. I rode the grey into the village to the British guard and asked that they close the Elbe bridge to the two horses, because we supposed that in the early hours next morning they would be taken to the black market, in Hamburg. I can still see myself standing before the guard. I couldn't remember one word of my school English and the soldiers didn't understand one word of German. But in the end we reached an understanding, they promised their help and gave us a permit so that we could remain out after curfew and continue the search.

'When we finally arrived back at the house we had visited, around midnight—there stood both the horses quite safely under their tree. They had returned alone and we never discovered if it had been a silly trick or a theft which had misfired. It was only certain that after their unseen return the horses were waiting for us, untied!

'With that incident our common trek came to an end. Three days later I drove the grey mare to my parents. My father had already hired out those horses which he had brought with him on his trek, but we kept the grey ourselves through harvest and the following winter. She lived on a small farm in a pig-sty whose entrance was so narrow that she had to be pushed in and out backwards.

'The other horses had to earn her food, but it was difficult enough to make ends meet. The army had already taken many of my father's horses, including some valuable brood mares, and we never got them back. Those horses which were hired out had a hard time. Those which were taken on to the farms and treated like the other horses, got over the exhaustion of the trek extraordinarily quickly; others which were overworked and underfed never regained their former strength. Our stallion went down with pleurisy because against the veterinary surgeon's orders he had been left out in a meadow in a thick fog when already ill with a bad cold.

'When we went to look at another horse we found him looking like a skeleton, blind in one eye and with a badly smashed hoof; during an attack of colic he had kicked it to pieces in the stable. The veterinary surgeon agreed with us that he could not survive the spring field-work if he remained on this farm. But in spite of this the owner refused to give him back to us. His own horses were also badly looked after and he was afraid he would never get through the work with them alone. If we went to the local authority it would take too much time if we hoped to get the horse alive, because he was not stabled in the locality to which we belonged and where we could have got help at once. So we quickly made up our minds to take him secretly out of his stable. But my father had a morally unhappy time in acting against the law—until we arrived safely in the evening with the horse!

'My sister and I had harnessed a fast horse to a light waggon and, at the beginning of the lunch hour, we were already outside the stable door, which could not be seen from the window of the farmer's house. I can almost feel my heart beats now as we entered the strange stable. It was a "breach of the peace" even if we were stealing our own horse!

'We had to go 1½km along the highway past the police post, which was the only way over the autobahn. The ill horse went bravely along with his fast companion. Then we bore off across a moor and travelled slowly home over unused cart-tracks. Later we heard that we had been quickly discovered and followed, but luckily not on the road we had taken. The farmer must have had a bad conscience and allowed our moral right over his legal right, for there was no chase. The horse recovered when he went to another farm and after the currency reform earned quite a lot of money for us.

'With another horse I did a journey of 50km to take it from one farmer who had used him badly to another. I took a rug, and a bag with a strap and my most indispensable belongings because I wanted an enjoyable ride. The horse was newly shod, but his hooves were in a bad condition and he was very weak; he stumbled so that it was no use thinking of riding and I could only lead him along carefully.

115

We had completed half the journey when we stopped at an inn and to my joy the horse received a good meal. After supper the inn-keeper cleaned a basket of turnips for him, and whilst doing so asked me if I wouldn't like to marry into his house as his son needed a good wife. It was an honourable offer, but I was worried about my answer in case the chestnut wouldn't get the turnips if I refused to marry! In the morning he told me again that I ought to think it over, but I had no wish to find the chance of my life here!

'A friendly farmer took the chestnut although I had been afraid he would return such a sick and sorry animal; we had promised him a strong young horse, which the chestnut was before we had let him out previously. The family were disappointed when I arrived with such a sad-looking beast, but they fed him well and he soon got all right again. I was exceptionally thankful that I had not to walk as well the 50km back to our village, as I had thought quite possible on my way there.

'In 1945 there was still no connection on our railway line, and almost daily things had to be carried somewhere. We drove a refugee woman to the coast, fetched my sister's luggage from Westphalia—all of them little treks—and we drove all over the land which was being used for troop manoeuvres in the heath, to try to find a smallholding or something similar for ourselves. It is due to these drives that I learnt to know our new homeland better than many of the inhabitants.

'I have admired the beauty of a sunset over the national park in the moors. The pines are similar to those at home, and I learnt even to love the houses, and if I may never return home, then I would prefer to live here. The people are extraordinarily independent, which isn't always easy

Page 117 The stallion Abglanz, one of the most prolific sires of post-war East Prussian horses

Page 118 (above) Swedish warm-blood horse exhibited at Royal Windsor Horse Show, bred on traditional lines; *(below)* the mare Kassette who took part in the 900-mile trek in the winter of 1945

Page 119 The chestnut mare who brought her owner and two small
children to the West, through many difficulties and much hardship.
Adana has just celebrated her thirtieth birthday in 1973

Page 120 (above) A new start at Schmoel on the Baltic Sea, Schleswig-Holstein, a stud belonging to Prince Maurice of Hessen; *(below)* fillies grazing in the peaceful surroundings of the Solling, West Germany

to live with, but the most lovable thing about them is that they have such beautiful horses.

'My grey mare recovered well during harvest and winter. One of her forelegs had become a little thick, as often happens with old horses, but she was quite sound on it. When she stood still she hung her head and looked very weak and worn out, and we often laughed and agreed that we would be able to get a night's lodging anywhere if we took the grey mare with us—for who could turn us away when she looked so tired? Once a man said to his small son, as we stood so wearily by the roadside: "Look there, that grey has come a thousand kilometres from the East." The little boy looked at her thoughtfully: "And since then she's had nothing to eat."

'But there was more life in the grey than one suspected, once she had warmed up she trotted untiringly and pulled as proudly as before. One day during harvest time, I drove her 95km, and the last 20km homewards she trotted freely and happily without wanting to stop once.

'But now the grey had earned her retirement, and we could not give it to her. We had not found a farm and in the spring I had to part with her. I couldn't trust her to be hired out for although I always got on well with her, she could be difficult. So I sold her. But I made a good sale, with the right to have first offer of a filly foal from her, and so they paid very little for her. In this way I sold her twice to small farmers, who were pleased with such a lovely animal and looked after her well. One boy learnt to ride on her and since has become quite a well-known rider.

'The grey mare was accepted into the Hannoverian Stud Book. The news of the collection and notification of the Trakehner horses arrived too late. I intended having her removed from that stud book as soon as her filly foal was born—but she only had one more colt foal. Perhaps under the Polish occupation at home her daughters are carrying on her excellent blood lines—for she had three before we left home. She was not made of the stuff of show horses, but because of her lovable character and willingness under every difficulty, I would have loved to see her filly foal grow up.

'She worked three years longer on the fields and faithfully pulled a milk cart; then she ended at the slaughterers. And I was glad, better this end than to have had her spirit broken through mishandling.

'The grey mare never came back to us on our smallholding because the work would have been too much for her. It was difficult enough for us although easier than I had at first imagined. But sometimes I become very sad when I see riders on lovely horses, because I wish so very much that my small son could enjoy the friendship of horses like the grey mare, as I did. It need not be on a trek and also not especially a grey.'*

*The writer of this account was killed very shortly afterwards at a level crossing. The earlier part of her story, another account of the trek, is included in my book of short stories entitled *Silver Spring*.

CHAPTER SEVEN

A New Home near the Baltic

AS I wrote in a previous chapter, very few of the horses from the stud at Trakehnen survived the collapse of the Third Reich or reached Western Germany. As they had belonged to the Province and were therefore owned by the State, most of the horses which had reached Mecklenberg were handed over to the Soviet Union as reparations when the agreement came into force that Russia was to occupy East Germany. The fate of these horses is unknown.

Some studs which were taken over by Poland do still possess the East Prussian blood lines and even have horses bred in Trakehnen itself although the famous stud, which now lies in Soviet territory, is ruined, having been largely destroyed by the advancing Red Army. I have been told it is used as a cold-blood stud. But of course very few people know what it is like east of the Iron Curtain which now divides this lovely Province.

Before he died Dr Ehlert, the last Director of Trakehnen, wrote to me that only a small number of the stallions sent out of East Prussia and thirty mares could be saved. They found quarters in Lower Saxony, Holstein, Hessen and at Hunnesrück in the Solling. He added that all the others which were captured were transported to Russia. So it was that at the end of 1945 the East Prussian survivors of the trek were scattered over Western Germany, especially in Holstein and Hannover, and were living under all sorts of conditions, very few of which were ideal and many not even satisfactory for the last remaining representatives of a breed of horses which now looked like dying out.

The owners of the horses were themselves also in a fairly desperate condition with no homes and very little money. They too were scattered about the country. However, they were still members of the Trakehner Society and so, in spite of every hardship their interest in their own and other people's horses never waned, perhaps it even increased because they had not much else to hang on to. And little by little news came of one and then another; how this one had escaped, and where he was living; that so-and-so's good mare had got to the West; that this or that stallion had got through; until bit by bit this refugee community had gathered all the information of the survival of their countrymen and their horses.

There is no doubt at all that Dr Schilke, now President of the Trakehner Society, did a tremendous amount of work in gathering news of all the members and in collecting and sorting out information about the horses. Dr Ehlert had found quarters at Hunnesrück and finally collected the remainder of the horses from Trakehnen there. At first there were only about fifty mares and four stallions.

There were, as far as I know, few surviving foals from the 1945 season, and there were none for 1946—also no mares were mated that spring. Their owners felt certain that they would need to make the journey home again and they wanted to be sure that their mares should not suffer as before when they were in foal. So they decided to have no foals.

124

But in view of the very difficulties which the horses had endured, it was very obvious that this breed *must not* be allowed to die out, for one thing is quite certain and that is that horses which underwent this month-long journey of life and death, under the severest conditions imaginable, and managed to come through, possess every quality which we require in a horse—for theirs was the greatest endurance test of all time. They showed endurance, versatility, speed, stamina, adaptability, fertility, had the most willing temperaments and lived on nothing. They possess everything which makes a horse an independent being and a co-worker and companion of mankind.

Dr Schilke had collected 600 names of members of the Trakehner Society (there were once 15,000) and he had compiled a register of the East Prussian horses—but he had to use a lot of persuasion to get people interested in breeding again. Even in 1947 no one wanted to have their mares served. Hope died hard, when at last it became clear that there was no immediate chance of a return to their lovely homeland, owners of good mares did allow them to be mated, and so 1948–9 was again a foaling season for East Prussian horses.

The arrival of the foals brought a new lot of difficulties for very few of the people who had bred them had land, and so the very urgent question arose—what was to become of the foals when they were weaned? The society thought out a scheme and a pair of foals would be offered to anyone who would take them and look after them; when they were grown, one was to be retained as payment and the other returned to the society. Posters were printed of a foal asking 'Who'll have me?' This scheme was in operation between 1948 and 1952 and seems to have been a success, at any rate it definitely helped to establish the breed again.

125

All East Prussian horses in Western Germany are now known as Trakehner and they carry double the elk-antler brand.

Under the Presidency of Baron von Schrötter three small studs were formed. That in central Germany under Dr Ehlert with 50 horses; another at Rantzau in Holstein with 20 horses, part of this estate being finally hired by the society. A private stud at Schmoel was formed by Prince Maurice von Hessen with 25 horses. Seven hundred mares were registered and 40 Trakehner stallions, but these included a number of Thoroughbred and Arab. There were in 1970 173 Trakehner stallions at stud. One or two are permanently stationed at the three studs mentioned and the others are out at country stations to be used on mares of other breeds and also isolated East Prussian mares. Sixty-nine stallions are owned by the State. There are now 1,600 living registered brood mares. This is an astonishing recovery and is an indication of the value of the breed.

No one can really imagine the sacrifice and the tremendous amount of work entailed in building up the breed again—no one possessed anything but they gave their all. The horses are all that is left to remind them of home. In fact, I am sure they mean home to many people. When one visits Hunnesrück, Rantzau and Schmoel on a lovely day in June, one feels very clearly that a little of that 'paradise' has after all, been retained. There are the mares grazing on pastures whose sea-shore borders the Baltic Sea—that same Baltic whose waters wash the coast of a land unattainable but never to be forgotten.

There are daughters or grandchildren of those mares who travelled so many wearisome thousand kilometres, from their homes to Schleswig–Holstein—those mares whose perseverance and stamina brought their owners to safety.

126

At one time the stallion Komet stood in Schmoel, now he stands at the State Stud, Landshut, Bavaria. His son Hessenstein stands in Hunnesrück. Komet's foals often take after his famous dam Kokette, who was born in 1938 in Trakehnen. The champion mare of the German Agricultural Exhibition in Hamburg 1951 and in Munich 1955 was Polarfahrt who at 26 years of age is now in Rantzau. And the equally famous grey mare Kassette (see page 118) at 29 years was able, until her death in the late 1960s, to enjoy her retirement with Frau Christensen—in Hellerholz, near Quickborn.

There are yearlings grazing in a wide paddock, as large and as green as the paddocks at Trakehnen—and the same sun shines down on glossy coats, just as it used to do there not many years ago. Quite definitely there is still a corner which is paradise for horse-lovers from East Prussia—and from England too.

One day a few years ago members of the Diplomatic Corps from many foreign countries were invited to Rantzau to see the horses. In the park the horses were paraded in the sunlight of a June evening, the mares and the foals led by the grey mare Kassette (1937), then the yearlings, and the young horses to be sold, and at the end the four stallions. The old trees, which have seen many changes of politics, threw lengthening shadows as the horses passed under them. And the men, who make these changes of politics, rubbed shoulders and talked together in the big paddock where the yearlings were our hosts. The Russian Ambassador and the Siamese, the French and the American, and representatives of many other races besides, were all there, admiring the youngsters over a glass of champagne.

One wonders what the future holds in store for these

horses. How will the change of climate and soil affect them?

Irish horses have plenty of bone due to the mineral substance of the soil on which the foal grows from the moment he begins to be formed, until he is born, and afterwards the grass which he eats continues to give him the bone formation which we require. In East Prussia the soil and weather conditions forced horses to be hardy and strong with plenty of stamina. Some people are of the opinion that now the Trakehner has moved from his native land the type will alter. For although the Baltic Sea bordered East Prussia, the country had an inland climate. In Schleswig–Holstein, the weather will perhaps be even harder on the horses owing to the maritime east winds, and doubtless the mineral conditions of the soil are not the same; it will be interesting to see whether the pessimists are right, and whether the breed changes in the next few years.

Having seen the excellent sort of yearlings now being produced I would venture the opinion that, if they continue to be properly managed, these horses will not change, and that they will grow into horses of the stamp of their famous ancestor Tempelhüter, the son of Perfectionist, and the grandson of the great Persimmon. Dr Aaby-Ericsson of Sweden who attends every Trakehner sale and is an authority on the breed, is quoted as saying that he could see no difference or change in the stamp of horse now being produced and that, in spite of their changed conditions, they are every bit as good as they were ten years ago.

So the Trakehner is established, aided only by moderate government funds. He is there by his own merits and the will and effort of the members of the Trakehner Society. Perhaps it is a pity that so little help was forthcoming and the society had to stand alone; for what a wonderful thing it would have been, if an established stud farm could have been put at their disposal so that the East Prussian horse could have had his own permanent centre, which in the years to come would always be his.

In Dortmund's Westfalenhalle there are two auction sales annually, in the spring and autumn, and every time about thirty-five young horses come up for sale, and go out into the world to prove that they are the best all-round horses. Once more Trakehner horses are being exported all over the world.

It is a bright cool day in November when I attend the sale of Trakehner horses in Dortmund. Most of the leaves have fallen from the trees and lie strewn faded and brown on the pathways surrounding the Westfalenhalle, probably the most noticeable building in Dortmund—the new Dortmund with its exceptionally wide streets and new buildings which have arisen out of the wartime ruins. Westfalenhalle is an enormous round building, housing a show ring, restaurant, stables and riding school and it is here that the Trakehner horses are shown and eventually sold.

Behind the riding school are the stalls, and it is a delightful occupation to walk round them and inspect these beautiful horses. The warm smell of horse and corn and straw, the satin coats and the interested, expectant faces in case a visitor may have a lump of sugar. Saddle, bridle, name and number stand beside each stall. And then one's eye falls on the animal of one's choice, surrounded by other admirers—she will be sold for far more than one can offer. Alas!

We have seen, during the morning or the previous afternoon, what every horse is capable of doing, in hand, under the rider and jumping free, and we have decided for which and what purpose each horse is most suitable. On the catalogue are famous names—a sire descended from one or

129

H

other of the great stallions, a mare who made the trek. This and this mare is right if we want to breed, and that gelding has all the qualities for dressage or jumping. Now, as we wander from the stables back to our seats arranged in tiers on one side of the school, there is a feeling of expectancy in the air; hope, perhaps mingled with a little sadness, from those who are selling a horse they have bred and trained; assurance from the prospective buyer who is prepared to have his choice at any price.

The horse is ridden in and goes slowly round showing his paces as the bidding begins...

They are presented to us—chestnuts, bays, browns and greys—young horses of promise, older safe mounts and mares who can be ridden, driven or go to stud. Bidding is fast and horses change owners.

And now the riding school is empty, only the be-flowered auctioneer's rostrum and the hoof marks in the peat remain. Most of the horses have changed hands, some at disappointing prices for the breeders, for one must reckon the cost of a horse's keep at least £75 per head per year. One horse will make the long journey to America, two will return to their old homes and companions; and perhaps as glad a welcome awaits them there, as awaits the horse who has been sold abroad for a very large sum, when he arrives at his new destination.

And so the sale is over, the lights are dimmed, the horses leave for new homes, some perhaps to achieve the highest fame and represent their country in the next Olympic Games, as did the East Prussian Perkunos, bred in 1943 in East Prussia, who helped to win the silver medal for Germany in the dressage contest in the 1956 Olympic Games with his team companions Adular (1944) and Africa (1942), both of whom have Trakehner blood. Another Trakehner

130

representative was Bill Biddle, USA. To these must be added the names of Bones, who so successfully show jumped for the Royal Scots Greys in Britain; also Vitez, who was placed first, second or third, no less than five times, in the great Pardubitzer steeplechase in Czechoslovakia.

We must not overlook Thyra, belonging to Frau Rosemarie Springer; Fanal owned and ridden by Herr Lörke and the stallion Polarstern, who went to Sweden as reserve in the Three Day Event (Military) Olympic Games 1952 and remained there, to become a successful stallion at the Swedish stud at Flyinge. Other well-known dressage horses are Poseidon ridden by that international dressage rider Harry Boldt, and Kassim owned and ridden by Frau Springer, who is equally well-known to American and British show enthusiasts. The grey gelding Spritzer by Famulus, has made his name and competed against those well-known riders the Kushners of the USA, at the Aachen Internation Show of 1966. Forstrat and Heraldik, both bred at Hunnesrück, were exported to the United States a year or two ago.

As the spectators and the buyers from other lands disperse my thoughts fly back to that other gathering of strangers in the evening sunlight at Rantzau. If only people would form a bond—just as the love of horses is a bond—to encourage the spirit of goodwill which is so badly needed in Europe. And not only in Europe but in all the troubled lands of the world.

East Prussian horses—Trakehner breeding—are bred today as always by people who breed horses for the love of them, and such breeders are the backbone of every breed of horse. Today studs, both privately owned and under the direction of the Trakehner Society, are to be found in many parts of Western Germany. I would like to mention a few that may interest horse-lovers across the Atlantic and the North Sea.

The Stud Rantzau lies in Schleswig–Holstein and is owned by Count von Baudissin and Zinzendorf. The Trakehner Society became tenants of the estate in 1956.

At first the Rantzau Stud served to help overcome those post-war difficulties already mentioned. It was the first collecting stud for those mares who in the coming years, were to make the name Trakehner once more well-known in foreign countries. That quite exceptional son of Pythagoras, the stallion Totilas, who was at stud in Georgenburg, East Prussia, and Osnabrück, Western Germany, stood later in Rantzau where I saw him.

Since the market today demands a percentage of Thoroughbred blood, this stud took on the responsibility of keeping Thoroughbred stallions, who were destined to further the breeding of warm-blood horses. If breeders are wise and use only the very best horses of the Thoroughbred breed with sufficient bone, then the high standard necessary to a warm-blood breed of horses will not degenerate. And of course, and this is important, one should not forget that the Thoroughbred breed of horses is not much older than the Trakehner warm-blood breed.

The late Herr C. Krebs from Schimmelhof in East Prussia, recently moved to Rantzau taking with him twenty-five mares and the stallions Preget and Garbenbinder. These join the two Thoroughbred stallions Traumgeist and Rosenberg.

Another stud which is directed by the Trakehner Society, is Birkhausen near Zweibrücken in the Pflaz. This stud was founded in 1755 and it provided material for other studs. Trakehnen also received some brood mares.

In 1959, the original stud at Zweibrücken was given up

132

and in 1960, the new stud was taken over by the Trakehner Society, and brood mares with the desired pedigrees were brought together here. The famous lines of Dampfross, Tropenwald, Morgenstrahl, Tempelhüter, Pilger and Pythagoras are represented by these chestnut mares.

The valuable stallion Carajan by Herbstwind, a 10 year-old chestnut, was chosen to stand at stud and, in spite of his relationship on the paternal side with some of the mares, his dam Cayenne VI provides a complete change of blood. His foals have the necessary depth and can now be seen in public. The second stallion was Ilmengrund, born in 1958. This young horse had the brown Humboldt as sire. From his dam Ilona and his grandmother Bergamotte, Ilmengrund provided a strong dosage of Thoroughbred blood. According to his pedigree his foals should have the ability to jump. The stallion has been sold to Württemberg and it will be interesting to follow his career. Perhaps he will return to Birkhausen one day.

The stud has a good riding school and youngsters are sent here from Rantzau to be schooled. The entire South German market for riding horses is supplied and also the Saarland and Switzerland, who is building up her cavalry regiments. There are 36 Trakehner stallions standing in Baden, Württemberg, 29 actually belong to the stud at Marbach, where both Arab horses and the Württemberg warm-blood horses are bred.

Another stud, Schmoel in Schleswig–Holstein, was leased by the Trakehner Society for its brood mares. On the expiration of the lease the Kurhessen establishment, of which Prince Maurice of Hessen is the head, founded its own stud, with a number of good Damfross-line brood mares. The first-class stallion Komet (see page 127) by Goldregen, stood here for several years; also the Thoroughbred Pindar. At present his son Loretto and Gunar, Komet's son, are at stud. Mares of the Famulus line with Arab blood provide 'counterweight'. Schmoel is regarded as a first-class stud, partly because of the good pastures which border the Baltic Sea and because of the management. It is well worth a visit.

Hunnesrück, taken together with Erichsberg and Neuhaus in the Solling, to which visitors flock to hear the stags bell in October, is situated in a very lovely part of Germany. The stud comes under the direction of the Ministry of Agriculture for Lower Saxony but is managed by the Stud Director, Baron von Stenglin, who lives in Celle. Celle is the chief training depot and stud for Hanoverian stallions; it was once the seat of the Electors of Hannover, later Kings of England.

East Prussian horses have been bred in Hunnesrück since 1946; particular attention is paid to rearing good young warm-blood colts for studs. It is due chiefly to the fact that Lower Saxony helped to found the central stud, at a time of chaos that followed the war, that the breed of East Prussian horses was saved. A number of colts with particularly good pedigrees are bred today in Hunnesrück. Many are bought for use in other studs.

There are about 50 brood mares, of which around 15 belong to the Trakehner Society. The remaining 35 mares belong to breeders from East and West Prussia, such as Frau H. Mack from Althof–Ragnit, now in the Soviet occupied part of the Province, and Prince Alexander zu Dohna–Schlobitten–Pökelwitz. No private owner may have more than five mares at the stud at the same time. Of course, such a regulation is necessary from the point of view of the management, but it can cause considerable difficulties for those people who cannot own land. West Germany is so overcrowded by its growing population and the millions of refugees, that land is very scarce.

In Neuhaus, which belongs to Hunnesrück, there are a number of young mares (see page 120). At first Dr Ehlert, Trakehnen's last Stud Director, managed the stud. He died in 1957. His head man, Bormann, who successfully brought a number of stallions to safety during the flight from East Prussia, was at his post until 1962. Hunnesrück is regarded as the main pillar of the breeding of warm-blood horses, therefore its main object must be to breed above-average stud and riding horses.

Another stud well worth mention, is the Trakehner stud, Webelsgrund, Springe, which was founded by the late Herr F. Bähre. It was built in 1952–4 on about 35 acres of good pasture. The 36 boxes are built in the style of Lower Saxony. Usually 3 Trakehner stallions are at stud.

Webelsgrund Stud owned the stallion Impuls by Humboldt, born 1953, and a number of specially chosen mares. These have contributed to the founding of a private stud which is really one of the best in Western Germany. Impuls possesses first-rate qualities as a stallion, which he passes on to his offspring so that these have shown above-average, not to mention first-class qualities. And as Impuls' young stock have been amongst the highest priced at sales, there is always a considerable demand for his services at stud. It is worth noticing that during the past four years, Impuls has produced such champion dressage horses as Kadett and Kassim. Some too, are good jumpers, like Sinus who completed a high jump at 2.15m.

Yet another stud was founded by Herr A. Nörenberg in 1958, at Rothensande, near Malente in Schleswig–Holstein. Both Herr Nörenberg and his wife are well-known horse-lovers. They have made a number of visits to West

Prussia, where they were received by the present Polish stud directors. Perhaps it is too soon to say much about the stud, although an excellent start was made by the mare Eszra who won at the Münich Agricultural Show of 1962.

Herr Nolten's stud has a second stud in Ireland where young horses are sent to be reared. The stud is too near the industrial town of Duisburg for expansion.

At Schick near Enzen, Euskirchen, Herr C. Bolton has been breeding Trakehner horses since 1953. At first the stallion Intermezzo, and later Kobalt, were used. There are about twelve good brood mares.

A number of studs have been founded in other countries, such as that belonging to the Countess Manzolini at Castelluccia, near Rome. She owns Kornett and several mares.

Frau Gerda Fredericks of Keswick, Ontario, Canada, has a stud of twenty-three brood mares and four stallions. She has been most successful with them.

In Buenos Aires, Argentine, there is another stud of Trakehner horses, consisting of two stallions and twelve brood mares, belonging to Frau Waltraud Burchardt.

Sweden has imported East Prussian stallions and mares over the years, for the Stud Flyinge. The blood of the stallion Attino by Fechtmeister is found in many top-class dressage horses in Sweden and also in Switzerland.

The chestnut Trakehner stallion Heristal, by Hyperion, who stood at Flyinge for many years, left twenty-five sons which have been registered as stallions. He also produced a great number of brood mares so that this blood line is very strong and the breed is becoming of even greater importance. Sweden breeds her own horses for all Olympic Games events and Flyinge is one of the most important studs in Europe.

The studs mentioned here by no means complete the

list, but are sufficient for the reader to see that Trakehner horses have acquired an international reputation during the twenty-seven years since the complete upheaval of the last unfortunate war. There is very little doubt that these very useful all-round horses will continue to do themselves and their breeders credit.

CHAPTER EIGHT

The Bells Ring Out

IN THE Autumn of 1958, I received an invitation from the Ministry of Agriculture in Warsaw, to visit the State Studs under its management. It was the first time that a woman had been given this privilege and the first time since the war that a British subject and writer had made such a visit. In 1964 I returned to East Prussia and again met a number of Polish friends. We generally spoke German. My visa allowed me to travel wherever I wanted, and thus I was able to enjoy great hospitality. (Trakehnen itself, now a stud for cold-blood horses, lies in Soviet occupied territory and cannot be visited.)

It almost seemed as if time was standing still. A hot sun shone down on the land and I felt as if a magic carpet had taken me away from all the rush and tear of our western world, into a quiet and lovely country—Masuria, a land of forests and lakes. Only in such isolated countries, can one discover a totally serene nature. There were wild flowers like the hedgerow rose, dragonflies, butterflies in all colours and birds, from the Great Grey Crane standing silent and still on one leg by the edge of a lake, to the Little Crested Tit, happily twittering on a swaying thistle.

Then we came to the horses, who were after all, the

object of my journey. Surely horses are one of the greatest bonds between man and nature and between man and his fellows? Whether one is a German or a Pole, an American or an Englishman, we all feel exactly the same when we look at a lovely East Prussian horse. The sentiments which we share are several thousand years old and are closely bound to the history of mankind. In Europe and indeed in the New World too, we all inherit a deeply rooted culture and a civilisation based on chivalry and horsemanship.

I saw how the studs had been built up again by the new inhabitants of this Province, with stallions and mares which had been found in many places: some in the Soviet army, some in desolated farms, some just wandering around and some even on the Kuban Steppes. Eighteen of these negelected brood mares from the Don were brought to Liesken, and it was with considerable difficulty that they were got in foal again (see page 107). The Poles had found horses from all over the country—no one who has not seen it can imagine the dereliction of the aftermath of war. But now the famous studs in Pr Stargard and Liebental, near Marienwerder, house stallions again. Weeskenhof and Diesken, once remount-depots, are now State Studs for the breeding of Masuren horses; in fact they are really a continuation of the pure-bred East Prussian horse, simply called by another name. The horses are bred on the same traditional lines with great care and with the same results in view, for the Poles are extremely capable and successful horse-breeders.

At Allenstein, which the Poles now call Olsztyn, we attended at 'international' horse show. The teams were all from Iron Curtain countries. Nobody from the West could or would come. A year or two later, due perhaps a little to my efforts, both West Germany and Britain sent teams. But at lunch on this particular day, all the tables in our hotel were decorated with the flags of East Germany, Hungary, Czechoslovakia and Poland. Our Polish friends were descendants of an emigrant Scot and I remarked what a pity it was that there was no Union Jack on our table. That evening our supper table carried the British flag!

An incident that I shall never forget happened at a small celebration supper given by a stud director, after we had spent a long day visiting several studs, including one for Polish-bred Thoroughbred horses. At one end of a long table sat our host, behind him the red flag with hammer and sickle. I was placed facing him and on each side were stud directors, inspectors and the two other women guests. Our host raised his glass and toasted his foreign visitors. I duly replied and thanked him for the kindness shown to us. Presently the man on my left, summoning his entire German and English vocabulary, said he wished to make a special toast and would we all rise. Then, raising his glass, he said: 'To Her Majesty the Queen'. I was very much moved.

On a rainy day in September, I attended the testing and selection of young stallions—colts. This was carried out with great thoroughness. I was given the reins and could drive a pair of grey half-Arab stallions, harnessed to a 'pirsch' carriage through the beautiful pine woods near Marienwerder.

I visited the stables in Pr Stargard, where there were 149 stallions 'at home' and there, and in Liebental which the Poles have renamed Kwidzyn, East Prussian stallions and also other breeds were paraded for several hours simply to please me, an Englishwoman—the first to visit these studs since before the war.

I drove, in my own car, through ruined villages and

140

towns, past blackened houses, through great forests and beside huge solitary lakes—through the homeland of all those people who had fled for their lives as a result of that unhappy war. Today refugees from Eastern Poland live in this Province and during the past two decades, children have grown up. Quite by accident I met several of those stateless Germans who remained behind; there are about 80,000 of them in Masuria alone.

In Juditten and in Liesken, I saw brood mares and foals grazing under a warm June sun. And I was told that the cormorants had returned to their island in the northern part of the Mauer Lake, just as elk are said to have wandered into the Osterode forest. I drove through Heilsberg, Mohrungen and Pr Holland; through that very district to which settlers had come, from so many lands several centuries earlier. Then, people of different traditions and languages lived in the freedom of this vast land of the seven great rivers, Vistula, Nogat, Passarge, Pregel, Gilge, Russ and Memel, this land of a thousand lakes.

Presently I came past the huge hollow oak and through the village of Kadinen where the crown prince once lived. There is still a stud here. I reached the Frische Haff at Frauenburg, where Copernicus was Canon of the Cathedral. And I stood at the edge of the little harbour and looked across to the mist-bound Nehrung. This stretch of water between that strip of land and the shore had played such a tragic role in the lives of people and animals, it was now calm, with small waves gently rolling against the harbour wall and against the little fishing boats lying at anchor.

The bells of Frauenburg Cathedral began to ring—they interrupted my thoughts of the past. The music of the pealing bells went out across the harbour, far away over the water. They offered a hope and perhaps a promise that one

141

day men would understand one another in this wonderful world into which we have been born, no matter what language we speak nor to what nationality we belong.

Bibliography

Burgsdorff, Wilhelm von, Director of the Trakehnen Stud. Letter to Count Karl Lehndorff, dated 20 December 1813

Deschamps, Dr Bruno. *Über Pferde*. Ullstein Verlag

East Prussian refugees. Their letters to the Society of Breeders & Friends of the Trakehner Horse

Europäische Osten, No 63. 'Millionen Heimatlosen Unterwegs'

Lehndorff, Count Siegfried. *Ein Leben mit Pferden*. Landbuch Verlag

Mager, F. *Wildbahn und Jagd Altpreussens*. Verlag I. Neumann

Oettingen, B. von. *Zucht des edlen Pferdes in Theorie und Praxis*. Verlag Paul Parey

Ostpreussische Zeitung, No 112. Article, Author

Rünger, F. *Herkunft Rassenzugehörigkeit, Züchtung u. Haltung der Ritterpferde des Deutschen Ordens*. Zeitschrift F. Tier: u. Zuchtungsbiologie, BII, No 3, 1925

Schilke, Dr Fritz. *Das ostpreussische Warmblutpferd*. BLV

Schilke, Dr Fritz. *Trakehner Pferde—einst und jetzt*. BLV

Summerhays, R. S. *The Observer's Book of Horses & Ponies*. Frederick Warne & Co

Thorwald, Jürgen. *Es begann an der Weichsel*

Wolfgang Weidlich Verlag. *Schlösser u. Herrensitze in Ost- und Westpreussen*